THE UNMENTIONABLES

THE UNMENTIONABLES

⊰A PLAY⊱

BRUCE NORRIS

NORTHWESTERN UNIVERSITY PRESS

EVANSTON, ILLINOIS

Northwestern University Press
www.nupress.northwestern.edu

Printed in the United States of America

10 9 8 7 6 5 4 3 2 1

LIBRARY OF CONGRESS
CATALOGING-IN-PUBLICATION DATA

Norris, Bruce.
    The unmentionables : a play / Bruce Norris.
        p. cm.
    ISBN 978-0-8101-2584-1 (pbk. : alk. paper)
    1. Americans—Africa—Drama.
I. Title.
PS3614.O768U66 2009
812.54—dc22
                                2009005765

THE UNMENTIONABLES

PRODUCTION HISTORY

The Unmentionables had its world premiere at Steppenwolf Theatre, Chicago, Illinois (Martha Lavey, artistic director; David Hawkanson, executive director), on June 29, 2006. The production was directed by Anna D. Shapiro, with set design by Todd Rosenthal, costumes by James Schuette, lighting design by J. R. Lederle, and sound design by Michael Bodeen and Rob Milburn. Robert H. Satterlee was the stage manager.

Etienne . . . . Jon Michael Hill
Dave . . . . Lea Coco
Jane . . . . Shannon Cochran
Doctor . . . . Kenn E. Head
Nancy . . . . Amy Morton
Don . . . . Rick Snyder
Auntie Mimi . . . . Ora Jones
Soldier 1 . . . . Chike Johnson
Soldier 2 . . . . Adeyoye

The Unmentionables was subsequently produced at Yale Repertory Theatre, New Haven, Connecticut (James Bundy, artistic director; Victoria Nolan, managing director), on May 4, 2007. The production was directed by Anna D. Shapiro, with set design by Todd Rosenthal, costumes by James Schuette, lighting design by Ann G. Wrightson, and sound design by Amy Altadonna. Ryan C. Durham was the stage manager.

Etienne . . . . Jon Michael Hill
Dave . . . . Brian Hutchison
Jane . . . . Kelly Hutchinson
Doctor . . . . Kenn E. Head
Nancy . . . . Lisa Emery

Don . . . . Paul Vincent O'Connor

Auntie Mimi . . . . Ora Jones

Soldier 1 . . . . Chike Johnson

Soldier 2 . . . . Sam Gordon

The Unmentionables was subsequently produced at Woolly Mammoth Theatre, Washington, D.C. (Howard Shalwitz, artistic director; Jeffrey Herrman, managing director), on September 2, 2007. The production was directed by Pam MacKinnon, with set design by James Kronzer, costumes by Helen Q. Huang, lighting design by Colin K. Bills, and sound design by Matthew Nielson. Laura Smith was the stage manager.

Etienne . . . . Kofi Owusu

Dave . . . . Tim Getman

Jane . . . . Marni Penning

Doctor . . . . John Livingston Rolle

Nancy . . . . Naomi Jacobson

Don . . . . Charles Hyman

Auntie Mimi . . . . Dawn Ursula

Soldier 1 . . . . James J. Johnson

Soldier 2 . . . . James Foster Jr.

CHARACTERS

Etienne, sixteen, black

Dave, in his twenties, white, clean-cut, athletic

Jane, in her thirties or forties, white, slim, attractive, no makeup

Doctor, in his thirties or forties, black, bearded, glasses, French accent

Nancy, in her forties, white, dyed blond hair

Don, in his sixties, white, gray hair, suntanned

Auntie Mimi, in her forties or fifties, black, imposing, French accent like Doctor's

Soldier 1, in his early twenties, black, French speaking

Soldier 2, in his early twenties, black, French speaking

STAGING

The set is a large upstairs bedroom and adjoining spaces of Don and Nancy's villa in western equatorial Africa. The house was built in the late nineteenth century but has been extensively renovated and decorated in a style that connotes American good taste, although some decorative pieces of West African art can be seen. To one side is a separate area with a table and chairs that can be closed off from the rest of the room by means of sliding doors. To the other side is a bathroom. The room is dominated by a large bed in the center, with numerous pillows, some covered in African tribal cloth. The windows look out onto row after row of palm trees extending as far as the eye can see.

The time is the present.

A NOTE ON LANGUAGE

In many of the countries in West Africa, people employ different languages for different transactions. There are countless indigenous tongues as well as, generally, a European tongue in which official business is transacted—a holdover from colonialism—and many people speak a form of English as well, even in countries that were not subject to British colonization.

For the purposes of the play, in the unspecified—and fictional—nation where the play is set, French is the official language of government and business, English is spoken for the benefit of the Americans (in its pidgin form by Etienne and in more traditional form by the more educated Doctor and Auntie Mimi), and—briefly—an indigenous language is used among three of the African characters. The language I have used here (with thanks to Amadou Fofana, of Willamette University, Salem, Oregon) is Bamanankan, a Malian language, which is not accurate to the region of the play and is difficult to render, as it is written in non-Western characters. If another, more appropriate indigenous language is available for these few lines and the correct translation can be found, by all means, feel free to translate them accordingly. I am only an *obruni*, after all, and by no means an authority or a linguist.

ACT 1

SCENE 1

[*Before the houselights dim,* ETIENNE *enters from the lobby of the theater. He is black, skinny, about sixteen, dressed in a filthy T-shirt and baggy pants, and wearing spotless sneakers of an expensive brand. He carries a soiled backpack, and a pair of broken headphones repaired with duct tape hang around his neck, connected to an equally dilapidated CD player. He walks down the aisle of the theater, stopping to speak to the audience in halting, thickly French-African accented English.*]

ETIENNE: Okay pipo. Siddown sharrup. Okay now. You leesen? [*To one person in the audience*] *Sharrup you!* [*To audience generally*] Okay guud. Okay. So. Dis show, okay? [*Gesturing toward stage*] Dis show you com, you pay to see? I sabi, o! Dis show, dey no guud. Serious, man. Dey stupid thing, okay? Whole show. Front to bottom. You don' like. True true. So leesen now. How much you pay? You pay big dolla, yeh? So tell you wha' you do. You go dere. Out dere? Window where you pay? Say dem to window, I pay big dolla, now dey tell me dey no guud. Get moni back, go home now, before

7

dey too late, watch TV, sontin'. [*To an audience member*] Wha? Dese pipo. Dey fucked up. How you no like TV? TV guud, man. Dey is Comedy Channa. Dey is Sci-Fi Channa. Dey is CNBC, MTV, BBC, Al Jazeera, CNN twenny-foah hour day an' you come to see dis? *What you thinking?* You think dey make you betta pipo? Smarta pipo den di pipo sit home an' watch TV? Why, 'cos you sit dere thinkin' yua big thoughts?

[*He snorts.*]

Tell you sontin'. Dis show? Dey like [*Mimicking hand puppets talking*] ya ya ya ya ya ya ya . . .

[*An announcement is made over the sound system.*]

ANNOUNCER: Ladies and Gentlemen.

ETIENNE [*re: the announcement*]: Who dis fucka?

ANNOUNCER: Thank you for coming to _____ [*name of theater*]. We'd like to remind you that the use of cameras or recording devices is strictly forbidden. [*cont'd*]

ETIENNE [*overlapping*]: Wanna take my pitcha? I don' giva shit. Take my pitcha—

ANNOUNCER [*continuous*]: Also, as a courtesy to your fellow audience members, please take this moment to make sure you have turned off any cell phones, [*cont'd*]

ETIENNE [*overlapping*]: *Wadda fuck, man?* Turn off phone? Who di fuck is dem? Dey *yua* cell phone. [*To the* ANNOUNCER] Fuck *you*, o!

ANNOUNCER [*overlapping*]: beepers, pagers, or chiming watches. Finally, if you plan to enjoy candy or lozenges during the performance, please unwrap them at this time. Thank you. And enjoy the show.

ETIENNE: Enjoi da show. *Enjoi to have a suck on dis, man.* [*To audience*] Who pay for di show, hah? Dis fucka no pay. *You* pay. Tell you dis. Sit in yua haus, watch yua TV, nobody say *turn off yua cell phone.* Watch TV do what di fuck you want, man. Who go stop you? Dis fucka? No.

[*The houselights start to dim.*]

Oh oh oh oh ohhhhhhhhhh, looka dat. Looka di layt. See di layt? What I tell you? Too late now.

[*In the dark, he continues.*]

How com you don' go, man? I tol' you go. You din' go. Now you go sit dere and watch di whole show.

[*Lights come up onstage. Late afternoon.* ETIENNE *sits across a table from* DAVE, *who wears a T-shirt, shorts, and hiking boots.* ETIENNE's *CD player sits before them on the table. Lying on the bed, propped up on pillows, is* JANE, *dressed much like* DAVE. *The* DOCTOR *sits in a chair next to her, taking her blood pressure.* ETIENNE *turns to look at the audience.*]

[*Murmuring to audience*] You fuckin' blow it, man.

DAVE [*to* ETIENNE]: Lemme tell you how I look at it. Give you my take on it. See, the way I look at it is, it's about choices, okay? Because we all make choices every day. That's basically all life is, right? Series of choices. For any given situation. And the way you approach those choices— See, each of those choices is like a little fork in the road, where you gotta ask yourself: What is it I want to do here? Do I want to do something I can be proud of? Or maybe not. Maybe you don't. And so what you do is you ask yourself, of these two possible options. Two or three. Of all these various options—

[ETIENNE *has placed his headphones over his ears and turned on music—which the audience can faintly hear.*]

Let's uhhh . . . Hey man. Do me a favor, let's— Can we—? Hey.

JANE [*to* DAVE, *unintelligibly, thermometer under her tongue*]: Dmvmvmphhhh? [*Tr: Dave?*]

[DAVE *raps lightly on the table.* ETIENNE *shuts off the music and removes the headphones.*]

DAVE: Thanks, man. I'm into music too. That's cool. But these choices, see, I mean— I remember, I was your age, okay? I used to want to cut class, you know, hang out with the cool kids and stuff. [*Laughing*] Telling guys like me to go *shove it*, right? I'm totally with you. You ever heard of Indiana? Place called Indiana?

JANE [*privately, to the* DOCTOR]: Wyezee nalken oooim nike eez a yile? [*Tr: Why's he talking to him like he's a child?*]

DAVE [*to* ETIENNE]: Show you on a map sometime. [*Turning to the* DOCTOR] What'd she say?

JANE [*to* DAVE]: I *hyead—* [*Tr: I said—*]

DOCTOR [*removing the pressure cuff*]: Yes yes. In another moment you will say.

JANE [*to the* DOCTOR, *privately*]: Weah, ees nah a yile. [*Tr: Well, he's not a child.*]

DOCTOR: But first. If you would try something for me. If you could, I would like you to raise your arms to shoulder level and make two fists, as I am . . . [*cont'd*]

JANE [*overlapping*]: No. No, ah khan dooweh. [*Tr: I can't do it.*]

DOCTOR [*continuous*]: . . . doing here, you see? I understand that there will be some pain for you . . . [*cont'd*]

JANE [*overlapping*]: No, not *sah* pay, a *law* pay. [*Tr: Not* some *pain, a lot of pain.*]

DOCTOR [*continuous*]: . . . but if you could—? Yes yes. Then let us say that I was to lift the arm *for* you?

JANE: Mm-mmm. No no no.

DOCTOR [*lifting* JANE's *arm*]: Very slowly. Very carefully. Just like this. [*cont'd*]

JANE [*totally calm, overlapping*]: No no. Peas doh doo dah. No. Sisley? No. If yoo doo dah? Otay ow ow ow ow. [*Tr: Please don't do that. No. Seriously? If you do that? Okay, ow ow ow ow.*]

DOCTOR [*continuous, lowering the arm*]: Yes yes. Good. Very good.

DAVE [*to* ETIENNE]: So yeah. So there I was trying to be cool, just like you, and then all of a sudden something hit me. And I thought to myself now hey. Now wait a second. Because you know what? I thought, hey, *maybe* Jesus Christ is a pretty cool guy too.

[ETIENNE *replaces the headphones and resumes playing the music.*]

Hey, man. Try to focus, okay? Still talking here. Eti—?

[DAVE *reaches over, unplugs the headphones, and takes the CD player.* ETIENNE *leaps up.*]

ETIENNE: *Hey hey big man!! Wetin dey do you, o!!?* [*Tr: What's your problem!!?*]

DAVE: Whoa whoa. Easy, okay? Take it easy. I'll give it back to you.

ETIENNE: Gi mi di Sony!! Gi mi. Is *mai* Sony, man.

DAVE: I know that.

ETIENNE: Not yua Sony. Dey *mai* Sony.

[*A cell phone starts to ring.*]

DAVE: I understand that. You'll get it back. But right now—

ETIENNE: Cos' I go show you, o! You sabi say? [*Tr: Because I can fuck you up! You understand?*]

DAVE: But right now we're talking, okay? Just being cool, okay?

[DAVE *takes out his red cell phone.*]

ETIENNE: Oh, yah, dey cool for you to tok on di cell, huh? Dey cool for you, huh? But not for mi.

DAVE [*as he checks to see who has called*]: I'm turning it off, okay? I'm putting it right here on the table and I'm not going to touch it. Is that cool with you?

DOCTOR [*to* JANE, *retrieving the thermometer*]: And open, please.

ETIENNE [*muttering*]: Big man no know im sef. [*Tr: Thinks he's a big man.*]

JANE [*calmly*]: Dave?

DAVE [*raising a finger to* JANE, *continuing to* ETIENNE]: But, let's say, for example, if *I* made up a story about someone. Story that *I* know for a fact isn't true. That's a choice I could make. And that's cool. Only problem, see, is maybe five, ten years go by. Now I need a job, you know, and I go to someone and say hey I could do that job. And this guy, he takes a look at me and he says well hang on a second. Didn't I hear somewhere Dave used to make up stories about people? Stories that weren't true? And what happens, see, is that thing I did all those years ago, that story I made up, now it's coming back to bite me in the rear end.

ETIENNE [*to the* DOCTOR]: N'ma fo I ye a be fe kan'ku tige. [*Tr: See, what did I tell you? He wants to bite my ass, man.*]

DOCTOR [*dismissively*]: Kari a ka di sa! I te sahali? [*Tr: Why don't you stop being such an asshole?*]

DAVE [*to* ETIENNE]: Want to tell me what you said? Because you know—the doctor there can tell me exactly what you said.

[ETIENNE *does not respond.*]

Doctor, you want to tell me what he said?

DOCTOR: Perhaps I will tell you later.

ETIENNE [*to the* DOCTOR]: Mogo kolondo, be y'o don. [*Tr: This guy's a fag, everybody knows it.*]

[*The door is opened by* SOLDIER 1, *dressed in military fatigues.* NANCY *breezes in, dressed in a country-clubbish sort of way, carrying two pill bottles.* SOLDIER 1 *remains outside.*]

NANCY: Knock knock. *So.* The situation *is:* There is Advil. And there is Motrin.

JANE: Ah. Is it Motrin *IB*?

NANCY: IB is bad?

JANE: IB is ibuprofen.

NANCY: Thus the IB. [*Hitting herself on the head, making a funny noise*] Doing!! And then *Advil* is—?

JANE: Also ibuprofen.

NANCY [*reading*]: It doesn't *say* IB.

JANE: Advil is always ibuprofen.

NANCY: My father took Anacin. Isn't that just aspirin with caffeine?

JANE: Don't know.

NANCY: But what *you* need is . . . ?

JANE: Acetaminophen.

NANCY: Acetaminophen.

[*She laughs, holds up a bottle.*]

> "I'm your Vitameatavegamin Girl!" [*Explaining*] I just mean, that's
> what the word reminds me of.

JANE: No, I got it.

NANCY: She was so funny. You know, what I loved about her is that she
was both funny and smart *and* sexy all at the same time and a lot
of people don't realize how smart she actually was because she was
so good at playing dumb, but she was actually *extremely* smart.
And, of course, some people are intimidated by strong women, but
I've never understood where that comes from. Jealousy, I suppose.

[*They wait for her to finish her point.*]

> I don't know. Remember in elementary school, you had to take
> those *tests?* Those placement tests? Remember those? Did you
> take those? Because I just scored *off the charts,* I mean completely
> *off,* and so they always wanted to skip me a grade, but some of the
> teachers, I could tell, they were intimidated. Saying things like
> *why don't we let some of the other children answer, Nancy,* which
> in retrospect, I think, was so *petty* [*without stopping, to* JANE] You
> know, you have one of those *faces.* Do people say this to you?

DAVE [*attempting to interrupt*]: Um—?

NANCY: And I have a *completely* photographic memory. Although it's
weird, with *names,* I'm like—

[*She makes a whooshing sound and gestures over her head.*]

But your face. It's one of those faces, and I swear it's going to come to me any second. It's, it's, it's— Oh wait. It's, it's, it's— [*With mock frustration*] Arrgh. Anyway, me me me me me. So wait, so *Tylenol,* you said?

[DON *has appeared in the doorway.*]

DON [*to* NANCY, *quietly*]: Honey?

NANCY [*feeling accused*]: What?

DON: C'mon.

NANCY: They *asked* me, Don. I'm doing them a *favor.*

DON [*louder, to* DAVE *and* JANE]: Folks got everything you need?

NANCY [*whispering*]: No, she needs Tylenol.

DON [*not whispering*]: We got Tylenol.

NANCY [*whispering*]: No. We have ibuprofen.

DON [*not whispering*]: What's that in your hand?

NANCY [*mouthing the word*]: Ibuprofen.

[*A different cell phone begins to ring.*]

DON: Doctor? You got any Tylenol?

DOCTOR: I can get you Tylenol.

DON [*to* NANCY]: How can we not have any Tylenol? Did you check?

NANCY [*displaying the pill bottles*]: *Yes,* I checked.

DON: Get Nonie to check.

NANCY: Nonie doesn't know where to check.

DON [*to* JANE]: Tell you what. I'll send someone into the city, back in forty-five minutes.

[NANCY *takes out a ringing cell phone.*]

NANCY: Well, don't send Nonie. Nonie's busy. [*Answering phone*] Hello?

JANE: Really, I'm fine.

NANCY [*into phone, with mock sternness*]: Um, *excuse* me, shouldn't someone I know be asleep about now? [*Looking at her watch*] Oh—well what *time* is it there?

[NANCY *exits. The* DOCTOR *begins collecting his things.*]

DON: Because that's just ridiculous. I know we got Tylenol.

DAVE [*stopping* DON, *to whom he is instinctively cold*]: So—excuse me—so Mimi *is* on her way?

DON [*looking at his watch*]: Well you know, people here got their own peculiar concept of *time.*

[*Beat.*]

[*To* ETIENNE] Mind taking your feet off that for me, son?

[ETIENNE *glares insolently at* DON, *then complies.*]

Appreciate it. [*To the others, as he turns to go*] Anyhow.

JANE [*to* DON]: And you know, we really are very grateful.

DON [*dismissively*]: Ahhhh . . .

JANE: For your lovely home. Which I guarantee will only seem that much lovelier the moment we're gone.

DON: Two weeks, then we start charging rent!

JANE [*reassuringly*]: No no no no no . . .

DAVE [*to* DON, *shakes his head*]: We've got to get some plywood up.

JANE [*to* DAVE]: Was that Patrice?

DAVE: Calling, yeah.

JANE [*to* DON]: We have to put up plywood. Where the fire, you know.

DAVE: Little rewiring.

JANE: But by Friday at the very latest.

DON: Because, you know, we got five perfectly good bedrooms just sitting here empty.

DAVE [*declining*]: Thanks. We have a lead on a place.

JANE: Well, "place," Dave, let's be honest, "place" is, uh—

DAVE: Temporary place.

JANE: Bit of an overstatement.

DON: What sort of place?

DAVE: Family home.

DON: Would I know the family?

DAVE [*almost laughs*]: I, uh, sort of *doubt* that. An indigenous family.

JANE: And not exactly *in* the home.

DAVE: Near the home. *Next* to the home.

JANE: *Behind* the home.

DAVE: Adjacent to.

JANE: More of a *shed,* actually.

DAVE [calmly]: It's *not* a shed, so let's not keep *referring* to it as a shed.

JANE [to DON]: *Functions* as a shed.

DAVE [to JANE]: And I never said we had to take it.

DON [to JANE]: I just hate to see you make yourself any sicker going back out in that heat.

JANE: No no, I just have these episodes from time to time.

DAVE [trying to seem casual]: And, you know, the thing about that heat, Don, is that we happen to be out in that heat every day. As are the majority of the people in this part of the world.

[JANE shoots a look at DAVE. DON is unsure of DAVE's meaning.]

DON: Yeah. Did me a little carpentry way back. Summer job. High school job.

JANE: Where was that?

DON: Tucson.

JANE: Oh, Tucson.

DON: Been to Tucson?

JANE: No.

DON: Seemed like maybe you—?

JANE: No. [Offering] Flagstaff.

DON: Flagstaff, sure.

JANE: Strangely enough.

DON: Cousins of mine. Flagstaff area.

JANE: But never Tucson.

DON: Well, Tucson's not going anywhere.

JANE: True.

DON: Because I—? You know, it's— Ah, never mind.

JANE: Ask.

DON: I mean, don't wantcha to think this is *weird*, or— Don't I know your *face* from somewhere?

JANE: *My* face?

DON: People ask you that?

JANE: No.

DON: That maybe you look like someone else?

JANE: You're the first.

DON: I swear I thought that first thing when I met y'all this morning.

JANE: Don't know.

DON: Or— I don't know, like someone from a *television show*?

JANE [*laughing*]: Me? No.

DON: And we can rule out Tucson. But it'll come to me. It'll—

DAVE [*to* DON, *indicating* ETIENNE]: Actually?

DON [*suddenly self-conscious*]: Aw, shit. Let's get outa here, Doctor.

DOCTOR [*rising*]: Yes yes.

DON [*to the* DOCTOR, *re:* JANE]: Patient going to live?

DOCTOR: Unfortunately, the patient does not allow me to say.

JANE [*as pleasantly as possible*]: No, I'm sorry, not to contradict . . . [*cont'd*]

DOCTOR [*overlapping*]: Or rather, seems to have concluded, without my help—

JANE [*continuous*]: . . . but what the patient is actually trying to do is *enlighten* the doctor about a recognized medical disorder, of which *he*, apparently is not aware.

DON [*to* JANE]: What is it, like the neck and the back?

JANE: I have fibromyalgia.

DOCTOR: And when a woman claims to suffer from this disease, inevitably a woman approaching middle age . . . [*cont'd*]

JANE [*overlapping*]: Yeah. Thanks for the patronizing tone.

DOCTOR [*continuous*]: . . . who is undergoing some *emotional* distress . . .

DAVE [*moving to* JANE's *side*]: Whoa whoa whoa. Is she in pain or *not*? Simple as that.

DOCTOR: Oh yes, she is *experiencing* pain.

JANE: Ow. Dave? Can you not shake the bed like that?

[*Around this time, the audience may notice* ETIENNE *rolling up one leg of his pants.* NANCY *reenters, still on her cell phone.*]

NANCY [*into phone*]: Well, let me ask. [*To the others*] Ashlee says what about Midol? [*Into phone, quietly*] Girls don't still use *Midol*, do they, for cramps?

JANE [*to the* DOCTOR]: Look. I don't know at what institution you got your degree. But let me say this—

NANCY [*into phone*]: Well I don't know. Then knock on their door and tell them to turn it down.

DOCTOR [*to* JANE]: Johns Hopkins University is the institution. [*cont'd*]

NANCY [*overlapping, into phone*]: Me too. [*Making a kissy noise*] *Mmmwah!*

[*She hangs up.*]

DOCTOR [*continuous, to* JANE]: And before that, the University of Paris.

NANCY [*making a general pronouncement*]: I'll tell you what the problem is. This is the problem with Western medicine: we treat *illness,* and we don't practice *wellness.*

DON [*a familiar disagreement*]: I— What the hell is that even supposed to—?

NANCY: *Other systems exist, Don!* Why do you think people like us are sick all the time?

DOCTOR: I am not sick all of the time.

NANCY: Maybe you don't know. How do you *know*?

DOCTOR [*shrugging*]: Because I am a doctor?

NANCY [*to* DON]: What about Shee-shee? *Huh?* Answer me that!!

DON: Don't drag the *dog* into it.

[ETIENNE *has raised his hand. When he speaks, all turn.*]

ETIENNE: Hello pipo? Ova heyah. I need go to make piss.

[*Pause.*]

DAVE [*to* ETIENNE]: Maybe you oughta try *need to go to the bathroom.*

ETIENNE [*to the room*]: I need go di bathroom to make piss.

[DAVE *indicates the direction of the bathroom.* ETIENNE *stands and crosses the room as the others watch in silence. After the bathroom door closes,* JANE *attempts to sit up a little.*]

DON [*looking at his watch*]: What is *taking* that woman so long?

[*He puts his watch to his ear.* JANE *inhales sharply.*]

JANE: Wow. Very painful.

NANCY: Anyway, my daughter Ashlee had a little dog she called Heathcliff. And then one day we took Heathcliff to the vet, and the vet said well I hate to break this to you, but I'm afraid that Heathcliff is actually . . . *a Sheath-cliff!* So then we just called her Shee-shee. [*In baby voice*] *And she wuz jush a widdle diddy biddy ding.* Wasn't she, Don? *Wiff a widdle biddy fuzzy faish!!*

DON: That was a cute dog.

NANCY: But she got so fat that she got arthritis and pretty soon she couldn't bend down to eat out of the bowl anymore. So we took her to the vet and the vet says— [*To* DON] And what an asshole, by the way, remember that guy? [*To the room*] The vet goes *maybe it's time we think about putting her out of her pain.* To which Ashlee and I say *ha.* So we found a holistic veterinarian who did acupuncture and homeopathic medicine and I'll tell you what, laugh all you want but after two weeks that dog was eating out of the bowl again.

DON [*to* NANCY]: What kinda dog was that, a shih tzu?

DOCTOR: There is only one nation that I can think of where not only are the people fat, but their *cats and dogs* must be fat as well.

DON: Ohhhh, don't start.

DOCTOR: This is the reason they must drive the very large cars. Because the people are too fat to fit in the regular ones.

DON: It's a cheap shot, okay? We happen to have a robust economy, is all, so if by some chance—

DOCTOR: Japan is a prosperous nation, and the Japanese are not, shall we say, *robust*.

NANCY: Sumo wrestlers.

DON [*dismissively, to the* DOCTOR]: No no no no no.

NANCY [*to* DON]: Remember meeting those Sumo wrestlers?

DON [*to the* DOCTOR]: See, you guys. You got a whole way of *thinking*.

DOCTOR: What guys?

NANCY [*to* DON, *again*]: Don, remember?

DON [*ignoring* NANCY]: A whole negative way of spinning things.

NANCY: Don?

DON [*to* NANCY]: *Yes. I remember.*

DOCTOR: They are just facts, Don.

DON: No, it's how you *interpret* the facts.

DOCTOR: If certain people have all of the power, who is to stop those people from eating all of the food?

JANE: Well, that may be partially accurate, but—

DON [*to the* DOCTOR]: Tell you what. Maybe spend a little time in the U.S. before you . . . [*cont'd*]

DOCTOR [*overlapping*]: I have spent enough time, thank you.

DON [*continuous*]: . . . go making these blanket generalizations, all right?

JANE [*to the* DOCTOR]: But: *Some* of us— [*To* DON] Sorry. [*To the* DOC- TOR] But I *do* believe that any person, any *progressive* person, re- gardless of *where* that person is from, has the capacity to recognize problems that might exist in the world and the opportunity to make some kind of tangible, positive difference, or, or, or, or . . . [cont'd]

DON:	NANCY [to DON re: JANE]:
Absolutely.	Who is it she looks like? Doesn't she look like someone we know?

JANE [continuous]: . . . or do I sound like some kind of idiot?

[The DOCTOR is laughing.]

DON [to the DOCTOR]: Glad to provide you with a source of amusement.

DOCTOR [laughing]: No no no. That is good. If you say that you can do all of this, well . . . that is good.

DON [to the DOCTOR]: Might've heard of something called *progress*?

NANCY: But you know, we are fat. Americans are just *fat.*

DON: Who's *fat*? I'm not *fat.*

NANCY: I'm fat.

DON: *Fat?*

NANCY [grabbing at her thigh, demonstrating]: Look at that. What do you call that right there?

DON: *That's not fat!!*

DAVE [to DON]: Well, let me ask you a question, Don. See, two and a half years ago I petitioned the District Council for a thirty-meter asphalt-paved drive for the school. That's all I asked for. Two and a half years during which— [To JANE] Wait a second. [Back to DON] —*during* which time I get to sit back and watch as a three-kilometer concrete-paved boulevard lined with palm trees magically appears connecting your production facility directly to the front gate of this house. Funny how that works. Meanwhile my students, those that can *afford* shoes, have to remove those shoes to walk through the ankle-deep *mud.* So, you tell me. Would that be an example of the kind of progress you're referring to?

DON: Well, Dave. I'll tell ya. You do raise an interesting question. And I think what you and I oughta do one of these days is sit down and— [*Turning on the still-chuckling* DOCTOR] *Jesus, what the hell is so funny? Can somebody explain to me what the hell he's laughing at?*

[AUNTIE MIMI *sweeps through the open door. She wears a combination of local and Western fashions—Chanel bag, shoes, sunglasses—followed by* SOLDIER 1 *and* SOLDIER 2.]

AUNTIE MIMI [*to the room*]: Very well. Now I am here. And where is the boy?

DAVE [*pointing*]: Bathroom.

[AUNTIE MIMI *snaps her fingers at* SOLDIER 1 *and* SOLDIER 2.]

AUNTIE MIMI: Allez me le chercher, s'il vous plaît. [*Tr: Get him for me, please.*]

[SOLDIER 1 *and* SOLDIER 2 *cross to the bathroom.*]

DON [*to* AUNTIE MIMI]: Took a little longer than we expected.

AUNTIE MIMI: I cannot control the traffic, Don, much as I would like to. Hello, Nancy.

DON: You pulled inside that gate, right?

AUNTIE MIMI: Yes yes yes. Please do not tell me about the gate. You are obsessed with this gate.

DON: Don't like leaving that gate open.

[SOLDIER 1 *and* SOLDIER 2 *emerge from the bathroom.* ETIENNE *is missing, and a window stands open.*]

SOLDIER 1: Excusez-moi, madame? [*Tr: Excuse me, ma'am?*]

AUNTIE MIMI: Oui?

SOLDIER 1: Le garçon n'est pas ici. [*Tr: The boy isn't here.*]

AUNTIE MIMI: Que voulez-vous dire, pas ici? [*Tr: What do you mean, not here?*]

SOLDIER 2: Il est sorti par la fenêtre. [*Tr: He went out through the window.*]

[SOLDIER 2 *has pulled three small appliances, tied together by their cords, up through the window.*]

AUNTIE MIMI: Ahh, foutre!! Ce'st parfait! Ils ont completement perdu mon temps. [*Tr: Goddamnit! Perfect. They have completely wasted my time.*] [*To the others*] This boy has gone out of the window.

DON: Ahhhh, shit.

AUNTIE MIMI [*furiously, to* SOLDIER 1 *and* SOLDIER 2]: Écoutez-moi. Vous ne travaillez pas pour cet homme, comprenez? N'acceptez pas son argent. Vous n'êtes pas ses employes privés. [*Tr: Listen to me. You do not work for this man, understand? You do not take money from him. You are not his private employees.*]

DON [*to* AUNTIE MIMI]: Hey hey hey. Easy.

AUNTIE MIMI: I do not know how much money you have given these men to bring the boy here, Don, but these men work for the PGED, and not for you.

DON: Mimi? I was just trying to simplify things since these two've [*indicating* DAVE *and* JANE] got nowhere to go tonight, and these fellas [*indicating* SOLDIER 1 *and* SOLDIER 2] were kind enough to bring the boy up here.

AUNTIE MIMI [*to the room*]: And who allowed the boy in there by himself?

JANE: The *boy* has a *name*.

DAVE: Etienne Mbegha.

JANE: His mother works in the vegetable market.

AUNTIE MIMI [*to* SOLDIER 1]: Connaissez-vous une femme nommée Mbegha? [*Tr: Do you know of a woman named Mbegha?*]

SOLDIER 1 [*to* SOLDIER 2]: Vous la connaissez, non? [*Tr: You know her, right?*] [*To* AUNTIE MIMI] Ouais, il la connaît. [*Tr: Yeah, he knows her.*]

SOLDIER 2 [*to* AUNTIE MIMI]: Elle est ashewo. Elle baise les hommes de la compagnie, et parfois PPEG. [*Tr: She is a prostitute—"ashewo." She fucks the company men and sometimes PPEG.*]

AUNTIE MIMI [*quietly to* SOLDIER 1 *and* SOLDIER 2]: Allez chercher le garçon et aprenez-le dans cette chambre. Essayez de trouver sa mère aussi. Allez. [*Tr: Go and find the boy. Bring him back to this room. Try to find his mother too. Go.*]

[AUNTIE MIMI *snaps her fingers.* SOLDIER 1 *and* SOLDIER 2 *depart.*]

[*To the room*] The boy's mother is a prostitute.

JANE: Well, I happen to know you're wrong. She sells *watermelons*.

AUNTIE MIMI: And she is a known associate of the PPEG. And who is it that spoke to the boy?

DAVE: I spoke to him.

AUNTIE MIMI: And what authority had you to speak to him?

DAVE: I think I'm entitled.

AUNTIE MIMI: And from where derives this entitlement?

DAVE: From *where*? Are you serious?

DON: Let's all just take a breath.

DAVE: How about from where our classroom and living quarters were set on *fire*? How about from there?

AUNTIE MIMI: You observed this happening.

DAVE: I was told how it happened. By the other children.

AUNTIE MIMI: I see. So, on the testimony of a few small children—

DON: Mimi, blame me. I said bring the kid on up to the house.

[AUNTIE MIMI *snaps her fingers.*]

AUNTIE MIMI: Don? If you please? You are my friend, but I will tell you when I am finished. [*To* DAVE] So. Based on the testimony of these children—?

JANE: I'm sorry, but where does this person derive *her* authority, huh? Not to mention the attitude.

[*Beat.*]

AUNTIE MIMI [*remaining calm*]: Don, I do not know the name of your guest.

DON: This is Ms. . . . uh . . . ?

DAVE: Adams.

AUNTIE MIMI: By the authority of the PGED, Miz Adams. That is where I derive it, in answer to your question.

DAVE: Democracy at work.

AUNTIE MIMI: Father Dave, you are entitled to your opinions. And because this *is* a democracy . . . [*cont'd*]

DAVE [*overlapping*]: Try *klepto*cracy.

AUNTIE MIMI [*continuous*]: . . . you are free to express those opinions at the proper time. [*cont'd*]

DAVE [*overlapping*]: Which never seems to arrive.

AUNTIE MIMI [*continuous*]: This, however, is *not* that time. This is the time in which I am trying to ensure your *safety*, so you may *continue* to express them.

DAVE: Great, govern through fear.

AUNTIE MIMI: I am not trying to—

DAVE: Great way to run a country.

AUNTIE MIMI: I only want to remind you of certain dangers, such as those that befell your predecessor.

NANCY [*as a gentle warning*]: Which we will not be discussing.

DON: He was just asking the boy a couple of questions, that's all he—

AUNTIE MIMI: Is this not why we have a District Council? Why not take the boy to the District Council?

DAVE: Two of the younger boys saw *this* boy. Climbing through the classroom window late at night. That is what they *said*.

AUNTIE MIMI: And you took it upon yourself.

DAVE: Well, I believe I have the *right*, if someone takes a can of kerosene *while we are sleeping inside*.

AUNTIE MIMI: Did the boy confess to you?

DAVE: He's not going to sit here and— No. He claimed it was the boys who had claimed it was him.

AUNTIE MIMI: And you have done nothing to give justification.

DAVE: Meaning what?

AUNTIE MIMI: You will have to tell me.

DAVE: Mimi. [*Listing the items*] We give them *food.*

AUNTIE MIMI: *Give* them?

DAVE: We give them *books.*

AUNTIE MIMI: Define "giving" for me.

DAVE: Athletic equipment. A safe place to play.

AUNTIE MIMI: Because I would define giving as asking nothing in return.

DAVE: Well, who pays for these things, Mimi? Is the council paying for them?

AUNTIE MIMI: But Father Dave.

DAVE: No. *United Mission of Hope* is who. And therefore—

AUNTIE MIMI: But it is not *giving* to make them sit in a classroom while you lecture to them about Jesus Christ, and only *then* do you give them a bowl of Kellogg's Frosted Flakes. I do not call this giving.

DAVE: I call it giving *two* things.

JANE [*to* DAVE]: Just tell her what he said.

DAVE: No. That was just, you know—

AUNTIE MIMI: What did the boy say?

DAVE: —juvenile.

JANE: He was provoking him.

DAVE: The only pertinent question is which one, or *ones* of them—

JANE: Just say.

DAVE: *No.* What was I supposed to do? Lose my temper?

DOCTOR [*chuckling*]: I will tell you what he said.

[*All turn to the* DOCTOR.]

The boy called this man a homosexual. He said this man had tried to kiss him.

[*Pause.*]

NANCY [*this is new information*]: Ohhhhhhh.

AUNTIE MIMI [*nodding sadly*]: Now I see.

DOCTOR [*re:* DAVE]: And just now, this man said to the boy that when he makes up stories that are not true, that this will return to bite him in the buttocks. At which point the boy turned to me and said you see, he can't stop thinking about my buttocks.

DAVE: Okay, well I guess we all think that's *funny*, or something?

AUNTIE MIMI: I don't think it is funny at all.

DAVE: But when it so happens that I'm *not* homosexual?

DOCTOR: It does not make you homosexual to admire the boy's buttocks.

DAVE: Funny. But *seriously*?

NANCY [*quietly, to* DAVE]: Honestly, half the people Don and I know are gay.

DON: Gay. Straight. Who gives a shit?

DAVE: Right, but for the record?

NANCY: People you'd never suspect. [*Beginning a list*] A congressman . . .

DAVE: But since I'm *not*? To which my *fiancée* could possibly *attest*?

JANE: He's not gay.

DON: No, no. We believe you.

AUNTIE MIMI: *But* I need not remind you of the sequence of events . . . [*cont'd*]

DAVE [*overlapping*]: It's not the same.

AUNTIE MIMI [*continuous*]: . . . that preceded the tragedy that befell Father Tom.

NANCY: Mimi? I have asked you politely.

DON: Hey hey. That's the past, okay? All in the past.

AUNTIE MIMI: It is *not* in the past. These people still exist. And I will not *pretend* they have disappeared.

NANCY: Father Tom was a sweet man with a nice smile and that's all that I care to remember.

AUNTIE MIMI: Perhaps you remember that they also called *him* a homosexual.

DAVE: Tom *was* a homosexual.

AUNTIE MIMI: Well, you are not in Southern California, and in some places this is not a popular thing to be.

DAVE: And that legitimizes murder and *mutilation*?

NANCY: Don?

AUNTIE MIMI: Of course not, but, if you will recall, he was *also* accused of something.

DAVE: Which was *also* a lie.

AUNTIE MIMI: And there was *also* a fire on that occasion. After which, as he was walking down the road late at night, and a car pulled up alongside him—

NANCY: *Don?*

DON: Uhhhh, you know, this is not Nancy's favorite topic.

JANE: Well, for the benefit of those of us who were not here at the time?

DAVE [*to* JANE]: It's— Okay: Father Tom. A few years ago, before I came here—

NANCY [*to* DON]: I have a very active gag reflex and I *will* throw up. You *know* I will.

AUNTIE MIMI [*to* DAVE]: Well, if I may offer some friendly advice.

DAVE: *No.* Just because a handful of violent . . . [*cont'd*]

AUNTIE MIMI [*overlapping*]: A *handful?*

DAVE [*continuous*]: . . . barbaric *criminals* . . . [*cont'd*]

AUNTIE MIMI [*overlapping*]: They are a political party!

DAVE [*continuous*]: . . . think they can terrorize the very same people who have come to this country to do them *good.*

AUNTIE MIMI: And they will not hesitate to use these children against you.

DAVE: So then, don't even *try?* You think Jesus Christ would say oh well, why bother to try?

AUNTIE MIMI: I think Jesus Christ never received a severed body part inside a plastic bag.

NANCY: *That— No. That's it. That is it.*

DON: Nancy's right.

[NANCY'*s cell phone begins to ring.*]

NANCY: I am telling you right now I *will* throw up, so consider your-selves warned.

DOCTOR: Ohhhhhh. Don't go *losing your head,* Nancy.

NANCY: *Okay, that's not funny!! Does he think that's funny?* [*Answering phone*] Hello?

DON: She threw up at her daughter's graduation.

NANCY [*quietly, into phone*]: *Ashlee, I'm in the middle of an argument, all right? And I am about this close to throwing up.*

DON: Had to get a new diploma and everything.

NANCY [*into phone*]: *Well then don't pick at it, that's why you have the prescription.* Now for god's sake go to your *class.* [*Making kissing noise*] Mmmwah.

[*She hangs up. Pause.*]

DON: Anyway.

AUNTIE MIMI [*suddenly turning to* JANE]: Excuse me. Have I not seen you on a television program?

[*All stop and turn toward* JANE.]

JANE: You mean me?

NANCY: On a what? On a show? A TV show?

DAVE [*quietly, to* JANE]: They're gonna figure it out sooner or later.

DON: I *knew* I'd— What show is that?

DAVE: Called *The Facilitator.*

[DON *and* NANCY *are thrilled.*]

NANCY [*with a gasp*]:
Oh my god, *Don*! Oh my god, *The Facilitator*! Why didn't you *say so*? Of course *The Facilitator*, we watch *The Facilitator*.

DON:
That's it. That's the one. With the mysterious millionaire who helps out all of the poor people? Now, *that* is a good show.

NANCY: That's a very *successful*— Didn't I *say*, Don? I said who does she *look* like?

DON: Do we get that show on the dish here?

NANCY: I knew it I knew it I *knew* it.

DON: And what's your character called? She's the millionaire's assistant? *Monica* something?

AUNTIE MIMI: Monica Chapel.

[DON *and* NANCY *ad-lib,* "Monica Chapel, oh yeah, that's it," "Right," *etc.*]

NANCY: So then what, so did it get canceled?

JANE: No no. Still on.

DON: See, now that's a show with a positive message.

NANCY: So, next season. This is something I always wonder. Do you get to have a *say* in what happens to the character?

JANE: Well, it's funny. Actually, um, I mean, the thing of it is—

DAVE: She quit.

JANE: I left.

[DON, NANCY, *and* AUNTIE MIMI *all ad-lib,* "Ohhhhhh, yes," "I think I read that," "I remember hearing that," "Right," *etc.*]

After the third season.

NANCY: Ohhhhh, okay.

[*Pause. All regroup.*]

DON: Some kind of money thing, or—?

JANE: No.

NANCY: See, when a show is successful like that one, I would think you could sort of name your price.

JANE: It wasn't money.

DAVE: The reason she—

JANE [*to* DAVE, *quietly*]: Let's not, okay?

DAVE [*quietly*]: Can't we explain?

JANE: Let's not.

DAVE: Can *I* explain?

JANE [*to* DON *and* NANCY]: I don't really talk about it.

DAVE: I don't mind explaining.

JANE: I'd rather let it drop.

DAVE [*to the others*]: Look, it's not a big— The reason she left was—

JANE: All right, because that show is a piece of *shit*, okay? And I guess it occurred to me that I might try doing something meaningful for a change, rather than waste another year of my life churning out mindless, moronic shit for the consumption of an audience of shitheads.

[*Embarrassed pause.*]

DON: Well, *we* enjoyed it.

JANE: Sorry. God, I—

NANCY [*privately to* JANE]: Oh, I say *shit* all the time.

JANE: No— I didn't mean to—

NANCY [*breezily*]: Shit shit motherfucker shit.

DON [*to* JANE]: And who's the fella plays the millionaire?

JANE: Um, Peter Scolari.

NANCY: He seems like a nice man.

JANE: Very nice man.

[*A cell phone rings.* AUNTIE MIMI *answers.*]

AUNTIE MIMI [*into phone*]: Oui? Quand? Connaissez-vous à quelle femme je parle? L'actrice qui joue Monica Chapel à la télévision. Oui, *The Facilitator*. [*Tr: Yes? When? Do you know what woman I am speaking to? The actress who plays Monica Chapel on television. Yes,* The Facilitator.]

[AUNTIE MIMI *puts a finger in her other ear, rises, and exits, still talking.* JANE *struggles to get to her feet.*]

JANE [*wincing in pain*]: Aggghh, it's like somebody took a red-hot *knife.*

NANCY [*to the* DOCTOR]: Excuse me, would you *look* at her? [*To the room*] Here she is in *pain* and he sits there staring into space.

DOCTOR [*pressing his fingertips together*]: Nancy, this *illness*, this *hypothetical* illness . . . [*cont'd*]

DON [*overlapping, to the* DOCTOR]: Oh, c'mon. Benefit of the doubt.

DOCTOR [*continuous*]: . . . which, interestingly, is never found in *this* part of the world.

DAVE [*to the* DOCTOR]: Oh, I see, so she's *pretending* to suffer from a disabling disease. Is that what you think? What kind of person would benefit from doing something like that?

DOCTOR: Uhh, an *actress*, possibly?

NANCY: *Doctors*. I swear to god. I remember one time I was stung by a jellyfish? [*To* DON] In Bali? Remember? [*To the room*] And we go to the emergency room and this doctor *looks* at me—

DOCTOR: Very well. Let us say that I *could* do something for her?

[*All turn to the* DOCTOR.]

· Supposing that I could.

NANCY: Ah-hah! *You see?*

DOCTOR: And only the symptom, of course, you know, not the *cause* of the problem. Because these people, they all say to me, Doctor, Doctor, why am I in pain? And what can I say to them? [*Shrugging*] I don't know. Life is painful.

[AUNTIE MIMI *returns, cell phone to ear.*]

AUNTIE MIMI [*into phone*]: Non, c'est la première fois que j'en ai entendu parler. Je ne sais pas. [*Tr: No, this is the first I have heard of it. I don't know.*]

DOCTOR [*rising to exit*]: Let me see what I can do.

AUNTIE MIMI: Don, what is this I am hearing about a birthday? [*cont'd*]

[NANCY *turns to* DON *so that* AUNTIE MIMI *cannot see her speaking.*]

NANCY [*through clenched teeth*]: Don't let her. I don't want her bring-ing all those people. I can't stand those people.

AUNTIE MIMI [*continuous, into phone*]: Chez-eux, oui? Ce soir, oui? [*Tr: Their place, yes? Tonight, yes?*] [*To* DON] I must assume my invi-tation was misplaced?

NANCY [*guiding* AUNTIE MIMI *out of the room*]: Oh, no no no. It's just a little gathering, it's just a few friends, is all.

[NANCY, AUNTIE MIMI, *and the* DOCTOR *have exited.* DON *watches as* DAVE *slowly helps* JANE *into the bathroom.*]

DAVE: Use my shoulder. Here.

[DAVE *shuts the bathroom door, leaving* DON *alone.* SOLDIER 1 *has been standing at the open door.*]

SOLDIER 1 [*quietly knocking*]: Scoozmi?

DON: Hmm?

[SOLDIER 1 *holds one of* ETIENNE'*s sneakers. He offers it to* DON.]

SOLDIER 1: Excusez-moi, monsieur. J'ai trouvé ceci près de mur. Cette chaussure. Elle était à terre. Dehors de là. [*Tr: Excuse me, sir. I found this below the window. This shoe. It was on the ground. Out there.*]

DON: Ah. Okay. Good deal.

SOLDIER 1: Quest-ce que je devrais en faire? Devrais-je vous la laisser? [*Tr: What should I do? Should I leave this with you?*]

DON: Right. Uh, je ne parle— Uh, pas de— Ah, hell, lemme think. Uh. *Not my shoe.* Uh, *pas de*— Tell ya what.

[DON *extracts his wallet. He hands* SOLDIER 1 *a couple of bills.*]

Good man. Thanks for your help.

[DON *pats* SOLDIER 1 *on the shoulder and exits.*]

SOLDIER 1 [*after* DON *is gone*]: Quels imbéciles, ricains bourgeois. [*Tr: Rich American morons.*]

[SOLDIER 1 *deposits the shoe on a nightstand and exits, closing the door. Low rumble of thunder. Without going to black, lights cross-fade to scene 2.*]

SCENE 2

[*Night. Crickets. The room is dimly lit. There is a light tapping at the door. It opens slightly and the* DOCTOR *peers in. Music and intermittent party noise filter in through the open doorway.*]

DOCTOR: Allô? Est-ce que quelqu'un est là? [*Tr: Is anybody in here?*]

[*He enters quietly, leaving the door open. He is dressed more formally and carries a cocktail glass. He goes to the window seat, sits, and opens the window slightly, then reaches inside his jacket and withdraws what is plainly a large joint. He lights it, inhales, and after a few moments pass, a toilet flushes. The bathroom door opens to reveal* DAVE *holding his Bible. His mood has soured. The* DOCTOR *stands.*]

Oh dear. Let me apologize.

DAVE: It's fine.

DOCTOR: The door, it was open and so I knocked— And I could have gone to my own room, but it is, well, some distance from this one, and now, unfortunately . . . I am in here. And I must apologize.

DAVE [*with a shrug*]: Not my room, anyway.

DOCTOR: Well, for the time, yes?

[DAVE *sits on the bed to study his Bible. The* DOCTOR *waves away the smoke.*]

[*Re: the joint*] Will this be a problem for you?

DAVE [*barely acknowledging the* DOCTOR'*s presence*]: Not for me.

[DAVE, *irritated by the noise, crosses to the door, closes it, then returns to the bed. The* DOCTOR *sits again and laughs.*]

DOCTOR: All of the people, you know?

DAVE: Mmm.

DOCTOR: It is interesting. If you were to ask me, are you a person who, in the abstract, enjoys the company of other people? I think I would have to say yes, bien sûr, this is only natural. And yet somehow it always happens that from the moment I arrive at any sort of celebration and I look at all of the people I had anticipated enjoying . . . I don't know what it is. I see them stuffing the food in their greedy fat little faces and talking so loudly and waving their hands and telling their little stories, and all I start to think is, oh my god, if only I . . . uhhh, what was the name of this *weapon*? It is a kind of stone hatchet that was the weapon used by the Native American Indians to defend themselves against the white people?

DAVE: A tomahawk.

DOCTOR: Exactly, yes. If only I had a *tomahawk* with which I could hit these people in their heads, perhaps then I could enjoy the party. Do you find this to be true for you?

DAVE [*without looking up*]: I don't really have an opinion on that.

[*Pause.* DAVE *is marking in his Bible with a highlighter.*]

DOCTOR: Is this not considered, uhhh . . . [*unsure of the word*] *desecration?*

DAVE: Is what considered?

DOCTOR: To make these marks. On the Bible?

DAVE: Desecration?

DOCTOR: That is a Bible?

DAVE: Yeah.

DOCTOR: And this does not constitute desecration?

DAVE: Not to my knowledge.

DOCTOR: Perhaps I am thinking of a different book. A library book.

[*Beat.*]

I would have thought you were invited to the celebration.

DAVE: I was invited.

[*Brief pause. The* DOCTOR *looks toward the bathroom door, then back to* DAVE, *and laughs.*]

DOCTOR: So, you were reading the *Bible.*

DAVE: That's what I'm reading now.

DOCTOR: No, what I mean to ask is—

DAVE: Ever read the Bible?

DOCTOR: The Bible? Noooo. I'm sorry.

DAVE: Don't apologize to *me.*

DOCTOR: No, I find it difficult to identify with the central character.

DAVE [*unamused*]: Up to you.

DOCTOR: No, what I was asking was— But I am interrupting, now.

DAVE: Go ahead.

DOCTOR: Nooo.

DAVE [*showing irritation*]: Go ahead and ask your question.

DOCTOR: Well, the question: Just now you were reading this Bible . . . [*gesturing toward the bathroom*] in *there,* yes? In the process of . . . uhh? [*Making a face*] While being seated on the—?

DAVE: . . . yeah?

DOCTOR [*laughing, slightly grossed out*]: I don't *know.* I don't know, does it not seem somewhat—

DAVE: Okay:

DOCTOR: —incongruous?

DAVE: I'm sure you don't need me to explain this, but yeah. God exists in the bathroom.

DOCTOR [*considering*]: I will need to rethink some of my activities.

DAVE: You know, just because a person is a *reverent* person, has a *reverence* for human life, doesn't mean that person can't also be— I have friends who like dirty jokes, okay? Use certain kinds of language. So what? If it's not *demeaning*? As long as the humor doesn't *demean* or *debase.*

DOCTOR: Do you like dirty jokes?

DAVE: Do *I*? Not particularly.

[*Pause.*]

DOCTOR: Because I know a good one. But it is very dirty.

DAVE: Go ahead.

DOCTOR: No.

DAVE: Go right ahead.

DOCTOR: *Noooo.*

DAVE: Why not?

DOCTOR: You just said to me you don't like them!

DAVE: We do have a sense of humor. People of faith, you know? And don't jokes supposedly function, in some, I don't know, therapeutic sense, as a way of confronting certain, uh, aspects of the unconscious?

DOCTOR: This one is about a man with an erection.

DAVE: Okay.

DOCTOR: There is nothing therapeutic about it.

DAVE: Well, if it's funny.

DOCTOR: His penis has an erection that will not go away.

DAVE: Okay.

DOCTOR: And so the man goes to his doctor and he says, "Doctor, my pen—" *I cannot be telling you this while you are reading the Bible.*

[DAVE *closes the Bible.*]

DAVE: There. Now.

DOCTOR: See, you keep asking for the dirty jokes, I think maybe secretly you *like* them.

DAVE: Maybe I do.

DOCTOR: *No you don't. Look how you are sitting with your arms crossed like this!!*

DAVE: Maybe *you're* the one who's uncomfortable.

DOCTOR: Yes, you are *making* me uncomfortable.

DAVE: Maybe you really don't like vulgarity and cruelty.

DOCTOR: Is just a *joke*.

DAVE: Guess you don't really want to tell it.

DOCTOR: *Cruelty* would be to *make* you listen to it.

DAVE: Suit yourself. No skin off my . . . posterior.

DOCTOR [*overlapping with "posterior"*]: *Ass.* No skin off my *ass*.

DAVE [*opening Bible*]: Whatever you want.

DOCTOR: Okay okay okay. Okay then. I think now, you are a bit of a *masochist*, but okay. So. This man's penis has an erection that will not go away. And he goes to his doctor. And the doctor says—

[JANE *enters, followed by* NANCY. *Both have changed into dresses suitable for a party.* JANE *now seems to be moving with no difficulty.*]

NANCY [*stopping at the doorway*]: I am so sorry.

JANE: It's fine.

NANCY: No, really.

JANE: Nancy? It's not—

NANCY: I don't know what is wrong with me.

JANE: It's not a big deal.

NANCY: No, it *is*. You asked me. You asked *specifically,* and I went and shot off my big mouth and it just popped right out.

JANE [to DAVE, *as she passes*]: What are you doing?

DAVE: What would you *like* me to do?

[JANE *enters the bathroom, closes the door.*]

NANCY: That is so typical of me. I swear to you, Ashlee wants to just *throttle* me, she goes *put a sock in it, Mom!!* [*Without stopping, lowers voice for* DAVE *and the* DOCTOR] Okay, I know she's upset about the photographer, but I am *not* the one who said anything to the photographer and am I crazy, or aren't actors supposed to *want* to be famous?

JANE [*from inside the bathroom*]: I can't hear you, Nancy.

NANCY [*calling out*]: I'm saying you can't blame them for being interested! People *like* talking to actors. I wish *I* was an actor so someone would talk to *me*! [*Without stopping, excitedly joining the* DOCTOR] Is someone getting *stoned* in here?

DOCTOR [*as he rises to exit*]: Is someone getting *drunk* out there?

[JANE *returns with a bottle of water and a handful of pills.*]

JANE [*to the* DOCTOR]: Wait. So, *how* much water?

DOCTOR: Twelve ounces.

JANE: Every three hours, each time I take these?

DOCTOR: I am not the manufacturer.

JANE: So three into twenty-four is eight, eight times twelve is . . . [*cont'd*]

DOCTOR [*overlapping*]: I only give you the recommendation.

JANE [*continuous*]: . . . basically a *gallon*. A gallon of water a day.

[*The* DOCTOR *exits, leaving his glass behind.* JANE *swallows pills.*]

NANCY [*to* JANE]: And plus, you have to admit, the look on his face was fucking *priceless*. Dave, you know the commercial councilor, don't you? Dr. Nguema or however you say it.

DAVE [*without looking up*]: I most certainly do.

NANCY: I swear I thought he was going to have an *aneurysm* for a second, with his eyes bulging out of their sockets like that.

JANE [*to* NANCY]: But you see what happens, right? How we wind up talking about some idiotic TV show when we could be discussing something *substantial*, something—

NANCY: What about the thing? What about the driveway thing?

JANE: That's only *because* you brought up the TV show.

NANCY: Well, what difference does it make if it's getting done?

DAVE: What driveway thing?

NANCY: I wanted to help and he said *give the papers to me right now, I'll sign them.*

JANE [*to* DAVE]: Somehow it came up.

NANCY: He's a *fan* of hers! He goes *we can't have Monica Chapel up to her knees in mud!*

JANE: *Exactly*, and that is not what I came here for.

NANCY [*to* DAVE]: Uhhh, *thank you*, Nancy!

[DON *knocks at the doorway. He, too, is dressed more formally.*]

DON: What's the deal on that cake? We gonna fire that up or not?

NANCY: Oh, keep your pants on, *you*. [*Swatting his butt flirtatiously*] *For the time being.*

[NANCY *exits.*]

DON [*calling after* NANCY]: And Nonie says let's clear off the patio 'cause it's gonna rain any second.

[*Awkward moment as* DON *lingers.* JANE *applies a Band-Aid to a blister on her foot caused by the shoe she has borrowed from* NANCY.]

[*to* JANE] Didja meet my buddy Jerry Swanson? Said he wanted to meet you.

JANE: He's the one with—?

DON [*jokingly*]: The *competition*. Big fella with a beard.

JANE: I did meet him.

DON: He's a good man. Rich as fuckin' Croesus.

JANE: So I gather.

DON: Buy and sell me ten times over. But I didn't mention the, uhh—

JANE: Thank you.

DON: 'Cause, you know, he elbows me and goes Don, who the hell is that standing over there in that dress? Where do I know her from? And I said easy, Jerry, she's just a schoolteacher, just— I didn't mention, *you know.*

JANE: I appreciate that.

DON: Where do I know that dress from?

JANE: It's Nancy's.

DON: Ah, right, because you know, you were standing there and he mentioned that dress and I thought to myself Jesus, for some reason I *know* that dress.

JANE: I'll say hi to him again.

DON: And normally I don't notice a goddamn thing when it comes to what a woman is wearing. Stand there naked, far as I'm concerned.

JANE: Well, I'll be right back out.

DON: You're welcome, too, Dave. Got chili dogs.

DAVE [*not looking up*]: Okay.

DON: All righty.

[DON *lingers for a second or two.*]

    [*Re: the door*] Y'all want this open or closed?

DAVE: Closed, please.

[DON *reluctantly exits, closing the door.* JANE *finishes her water.*]

JANE: Guess I'd better rejoin the, uh—

DAVE: Festivities.

JANE: As it were. [*Staring at him*] You're not going to eat anything?

DAVE: Not *that*.

JANE: I think I saw some coleslaw. Watermelon. I can bring you a plate. I don't mind.

DAVE: I'm fine.

[JANE *starts to go, opens the door, stops.*]

JANE: Okay, what's the matter?

DAVE: Nothing the matter with *me*.

JANE: Meaning what?

DAVE: Meaning nothing.

JANE: No, clearly meaning something.

DAVE [*as a diversion*]: How's your back? Neck and back.

JANE: Better.

DAVE: That stuff he gave you helped?

JANE: Well, I'd prefer to know what sort of chemicals I'm putting in my system, but, yes. Help*ing*.

DAVE: So, that's good.

JANE: I just mean, if these people have been kind enough to take the time—

DAVE: Hey, hey, hey, no no. Go on back to— Go ahead.

JANE: But you, you're going to— So, what are you going to do?

DAVE: Just going to read.

JANE: And if I go back to the party, then, the implication—?

DAVE: No implication.

JANE: While you sit here and *read*.

DAVE [*checking his watch and changing the subject*]: Really oughta start on that plywood.

JANE: The *plywood*.

DAVE: Thought I might.

JANE: Dave. Um, it's completely *dark* out? It's about to *rain*? [*cont'd*]

DAVE [*overlapping*]: Someone's got to deal with the plywood.

JANE [*continuous*]: It's over a mile and a half down an unlit road, and I thought Patrice was dealing with the plywood.

DAVE: And tell me again, why is *he* the one dealing with it?

JANE: Uh, he *offered*?

DAVE: While we relax up here in Villa Caucasia.

[JANE *closes the door.*]

JANE: Okay. So that *is* the implication.

DAVE: Look.

JANE: That the idea of staying here, even for one *night*—

DAVE: We were offered the shed. You rejected the shed.

JANE: Because the shed was filled with *goat shit.*

DAVE: And see, I guess I thought the idea *was,* I thought that once you were feeling better—

JANE: But if we're *here* now. As long as we're *here.*

[AUNTIE MIMI *knocks, opens the door.*]

DAVE: And you are *feeling* better, right? You *seem* better.

JANE: I'm . . . seventy percent.

DAVE: Seventy.

JANE: Seventy-two? I don't know. How do you expect me to *quantify* the—?

AUNTIE MIMI [*snapping her fingers at* JANE, *interrupting*]: Excuse me. Yes. There is a man.

JANE: Sorry. Two seconds, please.

AUNTIE MIMI: This is a man from the National Radio Service.

JANE: Thank you, not at the moment.

AUNTIE MIMI: Quite a nice man. He has five or ten questions.

JANE: That's very nice but I don't, as a general— [*Getting an idea*] Oh! Ah! However. Conversely. Would he maybe be interested in talking to Dave?

[DAVE *chuckles bitterly.*]

AUNTIE MIMI: I believe these will be questions pertaining to the entertainment industry.

JANE: Ah. In that case.

AUNTIE MIMI: And I would take this as a personal favor as the man also happens to be my nephew.

JANE: Then what about this: what if Dave and I speak *together*?

DAVE [*quietly*]: No thanks.

JANE [*privately*]: You don't want to?

DAVE: You go ahead.

JANE: I think *you* should talk.

DAVE: I don't think so.

JANE: You sure?

DAVE: You're the celebrity.

[AUNTIE MIMI *has been snapping her fingers at* JANE.]

JANE [*turning to* AUNTIE MIMI]: Uh, sorry, the *finger snapping*? Might be less than ideal.

AUNTIE MIMI: If you would? Quickly, please.

[AUNTIE MIMI *exits.* DAVE *rises to shut the door.*]

JANE: So, you want to just go. Just say fuck your hospitality.

DAVE: Nice language all of a sudden.

JANE: What you're doing is called being *rude.*

DAVE: Oh, gee, *rude.* Hate to be *rude.*

JANE: You don't want to talk to this person? Person from the media?

DAVE: Yeah, okay. So I'll talk about malnutrition and HIV transmission, and then maybe you could follow up with some thoughts about, I don't know, *Malibu?*

JANE: Okay, fuck you, Dave.

DAVE: Nice.

JANE: Just *waste* an opportunity. Let it go to *waste.*

DAVE: Do you *honestly* think—?

JANE: It is *conceivable* that there might be something to gain.

DAVE: Apparently so. Apparently *I* couldn't get the driveway paved. Two and a half years of paperwork. Little did I know.

[NANCY *walks right in without knocking. She carries a plate.*]

NANCY: *Knock knock? Is Dave still in here?* There he is.

[*She sits on the bed next to* DAVE.]

Okay, Dave. So: *Daverino.* You and I are going to have ourselves a little talk. [*To* JANE, *laughing*] Look at him. Look at his expression. Thinks I'm gonna roll him over and rape him!

[*She lunges at him playfully.*]

[*Seriously*] Now *Dave*. I am going to tell you something. I had *total* social phobia when I was a girl. And my daughter, when she went off to school, she sat in that dorm room and cried her eyes out for two weeks and was borderline anorexic and finally had to go on Paxil and that's a whole other story, but *Dave:* you can sit here with your nose in a book, you can hide under this bed for all I care. But I am delivering these two chili dogs right here to *the Davester,* who can eat them or throw them out the window or do whatever the hell it is he wants to do.

[*Beat.*]

And *then* I'm gonna rape him!

[NANCY *rises, leaving the plate.*]

[*To* JANE, *as she exits*] Oh, did he see the cake? I want Dave to see the cake!

[*She has exited, leaving the door open.* DAVE *rises to gather his backpack.*]

JANE: Okay. Yes. On some level, I agree with you about them. But *if* we have this opportunity, and *if* by virtue of my, whatever, *name recognition* I'm able to draw some attention to the very issues we've been— Then why not *take* that opportunity to— [*Noticing* DAVE *pack his backpack*] What are you—?

DAVE [*as he packs*]: No, that's cool. You wanted to be here. You said until we get the classroom repaired . . . [*cont'd*]

JANE [*overlapping*]: Please don't do that.

DAVE [*continuous*]: . . . which I agreed to on a temporary basis because I was under the impression that you were sick.

JANE: Which I am.

DAVE: So *stay*. You're "sick." *You* stay.

JANE: Very Christian of you, by the way, to treat people with *contempt*?

DAVE: I see, so *when in Rome*?

JANE: For one night? Yes.

DAVE: Yeah, if memory serves, I believe it was the Romans that *killed* the Christians.

[*Lightning, and a huge crack of thunder. Rain instantly begins to fall.* DAVE *drops his backpack, thwarted.*]

JANE: I swear to you. First thing in the morning. All right?

[NANCY *enters with a sheet cake, with* DON's *face illustrated in frosting.*]

NANCY: Look at that. Where's Dave? Get a load of Donny's face. Isn't that the *best*? You shoulda heard me trying to explain *birthday cake* to the kitchen people. What is it, like *gâteau de* something?

DAVE: Sorry. Yeah. Um, I don't suppose you guys have a cot?

[*Pause.*]

NANCY [*confused*]: A *cot*. [*To* JANE] What does he mean? [*To* DAVE] You mean, like what, like a *cot*?

DAVE: Like a cot, yeah. Like a sleeping— Like a folding, maybe, cot?

NANCY: You don't like the bed?

JANE: The bed is lovely.

DAVE: Or you know what? I'll just take another room.

NANCY: You don't like the *room*.

JANE: The *room* is— No, how do I—? Uhh. Dave and I. We don't— What I mean is, seeing as how the two of us aren't— Since it isn't really *official*.

[*Pause.* NANCY *stares.*]

NANCY [*to* JANE]: You're being funny. [*To* DAVE] Is she being funny? What, you think Don and I *care*? Oh for god's sake, we can't *hear* anything. Go at it all night like a couple of jackrabbits, as far as we're concerned.

DAVE: Well, I don't know if you're aware of this? But not everyone chooses to live their life like that.

[*More thunder.* DON *appears at the door with a cocktail for* NANCY.]

DON [*re: the rain and thunder*]: Whoa-*ho*! I think the official term for that would be a *deluge*!!

[NANCY *pulls him aside to confer.*]

JANE [*privately to* DAVE]: I really don't think it's the end of the world, for one night.

DAVE [*likewise*]: Well, I'm not sure I'm comfortable with that. Are you? [*Laughing*] Well, what am I saying? Of course *you* are.

JANE: Okay. Can I tell you something? The insults?

DAVE: No, this is good. This clarifies a lot for me.

DON [*to* NANCY, *audibly*]: A *cot*?

DAVE: Because, you know, I was *fine* with the shed. And you *seemed* to be fine until [*lowering his voice, re:* DON] suddenly some *rich guy* comes roaring up in his big fancy SUV.

DON: Dave, you know what? We got a queen-size in that downstairs room.

[*The* DOCTOR *returns to fetch his glass.*]

JANE [*apologetically to* DON]: Thank you. I know it's unusual.

NANCY: Nooooooo. It's *sweet.*

JANE: But Dave has his beliefs.

DAVE: Oh, *my* beliefs.

JANE: *Our*— I *share* his beliefs. And how often do you meet a man who has *any?*

NANCY: Oh, men are the *pits.*

DAVE: Well, as long as something is explicitly forbidden by scripture?

DON: I wouldn't say *all* men are the pits.

NANCY [*in baby voice*]: *Not yew. I wuddent tawking about yewwww.*

[*She kisses him several times.*]

DOCTOR [*about to exit again, stopping at* DAVE's *comment*]: What about scripture?

DAVE: It's not a big deal. I've slept on floors, okay? I've slept on *dirt.*

DON: Tell you, though. I've slept on that queen-size and that is a comfortable mattress.

DOCTOR [*quietly, to* DAVE]: May I ask—?

NANCY: Nooo, I think it's *romantic.* I'm *jealous.* [*Sitting*] I mean, when you think of all the men I used to . . . *you know.* Should've been a revolving door at the foot of my bed, and where did all *that* get me? [*Re:* DON] Well, okay, it got me *this big stud right here.* But some people aren't *like* that and that is *fine* and that is what is so *great* about the world. Some people . . . [*settling into a story*] well, all right, my first husband? Roger was different from Donny, you know, lying there snoring like a sack of Idaho potatoes. Needed a *cattle prod* for *that* one, let me tell you, just to get a few measly seconds of physical affection, but frankly, I wasn't ready to check into a *convent* at that point. [*To* DON] Wait. [*To the others*] On the other hand.

DON: Nance?

NANCY: Some people. [*Re:* DAVE *and* JANE] These two have a *spiritual* thing. And maybe that was Roger's thing. Hell if I know. And god bless Roger. If not for Roger I wouldn't have my Ashlee, and Ashlee is like her father that way. Ashlee loves to go *I'm not a pig like you, Mom!* Oh-ho, that girl has a *mouth* on her. *You'd be happy living in a mud puddle as long as they feed you and fuck you every now and then!* And you know what I say back to her? I say Ashlee? Oink oink oink.

DON [*to* NANCY]: You're spilling your drink.

NANCY [*defensively*]: I'm not *drunk.*

DON: I said you're *spilling.*

NANCY: *That'll come out.* [*To* JANE] Don't you love that carpet? That was handmade in Marrakech.

[AUNTIE MIMI *enters with a purse and umbrella.*]

AUNTIE MIMI: Miz Adams. My nephew has given me this card with a telephone number and I have assured him that you will be calling him, and if you should choose not to do so . . . [*cont'd*]

JANE [*overlapping*]: Okay. Yes. I can't guarantee, but—

AUNTIE MIMI [*continuous*]: . . . I believe he will consider it somewhat insulting. And now, Don, I will say good night.

DON: No hurry.

AUNTIE MIMI: Thank you, no. The car is waiting for me.

[DAVE *resumes filling his backpack.*]

DOCTOR [*to* DAVE]: But if I may? As concerns the sex act outside of the marriage? There is a . . . proscription, yes?

AUNTIE MIMI [*to* NANCY, *stopping on her way out*]: *What* is the topic?

DAVE [*as he packs*]: Yep. That's what we teach. We teach abstinence.

NANCY [*to* DON]: Boy did I ever flunk *that* class!!

DOCTOR: And you apply these principles to yourself, as well?

DAVE: You asking am I a hypocrite? No, I'm not a hypocrite. I teach by example.

DOCTOR: Have you *been* married?

JANE: *I* was married.

NANCY: Ohhhh!

JANE: To a *coke fiend*, but—

NANCY: Don and I got married in a *balloon.* [*To* DON] Wasn't that a *hoot*? Wasn't that *fun*?

DOCTOR [*refusing to let it drop*]: Yes, but if *he* has *not* been married, and if the sex act outside of the marital context constitutes . . . ehh, what is the word, uh, *fornication*? Yes?

NANCY [*to the* DOCTOR]: Wait. Time-out. Start over.

DOCTOR [*slowly*]: He says: He is opposed to fornication. And *if* this is so, and if he has never *been* married, then, may not one reasonably conclude that he, himself, has never, uhh . . . ?

[*Pause. Then, simultaneously.*]

NANCY	DON:	AUNTIE MIMI	DOCTOR:
[*dismissively*]: Oh *god*. Oh *noooo*.	Oh, that is not what he *meant*. Jesus Christ. Cut it out.	[*laughing*]: Ohhhhh no no no. That is not . . . noooo.	I'm sorry. I'm *sorry*. I was only asking.

[*Long pause. All wonder.*]

DON [*trying to end the discussion*]: Actually, I don't know *what* he meant, but—

DAVE: So what if that *is* what I meant? You think I should be *embarrassed*?

[*All stare.*]

NANCY	DON:	AUNTIE MIMI	DOCTOR:
[*kindly*]: Not at all. No. Not. At. All.	Nooooooo. Hell, no. What the hell business is it of ours in the first place?	[*laughing*]: No, no, no! I will not believe it! He is making it all up.	No one said that! Who said that you should be embarrassed?

JANE [*halfheartedly coming to his defense*]: As I've said. Dave has his beliefs.

DAVE: Once again.

JANE: *We* have these beliefs. And what is the point of having beliefs if if if if—?

DOCTOR: May I ask one more—?

DON [*sensing trouble*]: No, no, now let's just let the whole thing—

DAVE [*defiantly*]: Ask whatever you want.

DOCTOR: Well, would this extend to . . . erm, *all* activities, premaritally speaking?

NANCY [*to the* DOCTOR]: *Shhhhhh!!! Oh god, don't.*

DAVE: Oral sex? Is that your question?

DON [*to the* DOCTOR]: How on earth is *any* of this *any* of our goddamn *business?*

DOCTOR [*overlapping* DON, *innocently*]: I am a doctor. I am curious.

DAVE: Yeah, oral sex is out. *All* sex, actually. Anybody else? Now's your chance.

DON [*apologetically*]: Dave, listen.

DAVE: Any more comments about my supposed lack of virility?

[*All respond simultaneously with variations on "no."*]

DOCTOR: Father Dave. No one has questioned your *virility.*

AUNTIE MIMI [*out of the side of her mouth*]: But it is a word that *starts with v.*

[NANCY, *the* DOCTOR, *and* AUNTIE MIMI *try to suppress their laughter.*]

DON: Dave, I don't know what's wrong with these people.

DAVE: No, it's about what I expect.

NANCY: Starts with *v* and rhymes with *sturgeon.*

[*The laughing escalates.*]

DOCTOR: *But at least he is not gay.*

DON: Aw, shut the hell up.

DAVE: About what I expect from people who are the moral equivalent of pimps and murderers.

JANE:	DON:
Dave!	Well now, hang on.

DAVE: Wanna meet some of my students, Don? The twelve-year-old girls who support their families by selling their bodies to the men who work at your facility? I'll introduce you.

AUNTIE MIMI: Oh dear oh dear oh dear.

DAVE: And why do the families need money? *Maybe* it's because you displaced them from their land and their traditional livelihoods and gave them nothing in return.

DON [*trying to be reasonable*]: I believe they got something called *jobs.*

DAVE: They *had* jobs, Don. Fishing? Farming? Not now. Now they get to work for *you* in a facility so toxic, so deadly, you had to find some powerless third-world backwater nation with a government of *unelected amoral gangsters* . . . [*cont'd*]

AUNTIE MIMI [*overlapping*]: That is *enough.* Now you have said *enough.*

DAVE [*continuous*]: . . . who you can pay off to look the other way as you systematically poison a population of expendable dark-skinned people.

JANE: *Dave!*

NANCY [*to* DON]: Oh, and happy birthday, by the way.

DON: You know, half that stuff has never been proven.

DAVE [*pointing at* AUNTIE MIMI]: *Because her government suppressed further testing!* Want to talk about the fourfold rise in cancer deaths? [*Counting off a list*] The concentration of atmospheric mercury downwind of the plant? The arsenic in the groundwater? How about the forty percent spike in infant mortality within a three-mile radius of the production facility? Explain any one of those. Your choice.

AUNTIE MIMI [*furiously*]: *Donald Butler is a hero to the people of this country. You, on the other hand—*

DAVE: Oh right. That's right. The people of this country are all *celebrating* the man who sits up here in this grotesque plantation. Right. [*cont'd*]

NANCY [*overlapping*]: Grotesque. Huh.

DAVE [*continuous*]: While they make fifteen cents an hour and wade through puddles of raw sewage not half a mile from his tennis court and his twelve-foot walls topped with razor wire. Ever stop and wonder why all of the children *spit* on your car when you drive by, Don? Sorry, but they *despise you.* [*Re:* AUNTIE MIMI] Almost as much as they despise her so-called government.

[*Horrible pause.*]

JANE [*to* DON *and* NANCY]: I am so sorry.

DAVE: Don't apologize for me.

DON [*to* DAVE]: Well, I know you think I don't understand. But I'd *like* to understand.

DAVE: How, Don? How can you understand the position of the people I minister to when you have all of *this* in the way, huh? What were Jesus's words? Recall something about "the eye of a needle"?

[*At mention of Jesus, all groan.*]

NANCY: Oh boy.

JANE [*to* DAVE, *quietly*]: Can we maybe ease up on the whole *Jesus* thing?

DAVE: Oh, you want *easy* Jesus? The version where he didn't really *mean* all of that stuff? Well, guess what? *There is no easy version.* And that is why you will never understand the people we work with, Don. The position of the people who are working and dying for *you.*

DON: I'm *trying* to understand.

DAVE: Please. You can't even understand *my* position.

DOCTOR: Would that be the *missionary* position?

[*Try as they might,* NANCY, AUNTIE MIMI, *the* DOCTOR, *and* JANE *cannot conceal their laughter. Only* DON *does not laugh.* DAVE *dons his backpack and a plastic poncho.*]

JANE: Dave don't. Dave?

DAVE [*to* JANE, *quietly*]: Do what you want. I'm sure you'll be very happy.

NANCY [*from trying to suppress her laughter*]: *Oh god. My drink's coming out of my nose.*

[DAVE *picks up a guitar in a case and makes for the door as the others laugh.*]

DON: Awww, c'mon. Don't do that.

DAVE [*like a threat*]: You know something? I'm going to say a prayer for every single one of— *No I'm not. You can all rot in hell.*

[DAVE *exits, with* JANE *following. The* DOCTOR, NANCY, *and* AUNTIE MIMI *are still laughing.*]

JANE [*as she follows* DAVE *out*]: Dave *stop it*. Could you just— *Shit.*

DON [*to the others*]: What the hell is—? I'm ashamed of the whole *bunch* of you.

AUNTIE MIMI: Oh, Don.

DON: Well, the way I was brought up is, if I take the trouble to invite some folks into my *home*—

AUNTIE MIMI: Father Dave is one of these people who love to be outraged.

DON: What about the young woman?

NANCY: Not *that* young.

DON: And whatever you may think. Whatever your opinion might be.

AUNTIE MIMI [*anger rising*]: You let him *insult* you.

DON: Well, that's *my* problem, isn't it?

AUNTIE MIMI: But when he insults *me,* then it is *my* problem.

NANCY [*still enjoying it*]: *The missionary position!*

AUNTIE MIMI [*anger erupting*]: To my *face.* For *three* years now, insulting me to my *face* with this incessant denigration of the PGED.

DON: Gee whiz, why not have him *deported?*

AUNTIE MIMI: Don't think it has not been considered.

DON: If his little cinder block shack of a classroom is such a *terrible threat* to this nation? Just have him *shot,* why don'tcha?

AUNTIE MIMI: That, too, is an option.

DON: Handing out chocolate chip cookies and miniature Bibles to these little barefoot illiterate kids, if you think that's somehow gonna *bring down the government*—?

AUNTIE MIMI: He is against *you*, Don. Not me. It is *you* he would bring down. They are *your* future workers, whose tiny little brains he is attempting to turn against *you*!

DON [*with finality*]: *I don't care who he is or what he does as long as he is a guest here in this house!*

DOCTOR [*to* DON]: All right. Time to relax.

AUNTIE MIMI [*quietly, as she gathers her things*]: I do not appreciate your tone of voice, Don. Not at all.

NANCY [*taking* DON's *arm*]: Come on. Come on, *birthday boy.*

[AUNTIE MIMI *exits.*]

DON [*to* NANCY]: Stop it. [*To* AUNTIE MIMI, *as she exits*] That is *not* how I was raised and that's all there is to it.

NANCY [*suggestively*]: *I* know what this birthday boy needs.

DON: I said *cut it out,* goddamnit.

NANCY: Ohhhhh*kay.*

DON [*to* NANCY, *as kindly as possible*]: And I'll tell you something else, honey. You keep going on and on and on like that all the time while no one else is talking. I know you think you're being entertaining or funny or something, but I gotta tell you, when I hear you doing that, sometimes, to *my* way of thinking, you don't come off sounding all that bright.

[DON *has crossed a line with* NANCY.]

NANCY [*coldly, insulted*]: Is that right?

DON: Doesn't kill a person to *listen* every now and then.

NANCY: Not that *bright.*

DON: Maybe somebody else has an interesting point of view. But how do you ever expect to know if you don't give them half a chance?

NANCY: Guess I'm just not *bright* enough.

DON: Ah, cut it out.

NANCY: Wait, cut *what* out? I'm not very *bright*.

DON: Sit there thinking you sound all *erudite* or something—

NANCY: Wait wait. *E-r*— Can you *spell* that for me?

DON [*quietly dismissive*]: Ahhh, *fuck off,* Nance.

NANCY: Mm-hm. With pleasure, *buster.*

[NANCY *exits, leaving* DON *and the* DOCTOR. DON *sits.*]

DON [*to himself*]: Goddamnit.

DOCTOR: Soooo. How are we feeling, Don?

DON: Why the hell did I eat all that shit? Chili dogs and chocolate cake like a goddamn ten-year-old kid. Next time why don't you remind me not to go and eat a pile of shit like that?

DOCTOR: I did remind you.

[JANE *returns, drenched head to toe.*]

DON: Oh. Hey.

JANE: Don't say it.

DON: No.

JANE: He was in the wrong.

DON: No.

JANE: He had absolutely no right to take it out on you. *But:*

DON: Dave's a good man.

DOCTOR: Don?

JANE: None of which changes the fact that Dave . . . [*cont'd*]

DON [*overlapping*]: Can we get you a towel, or—?

JANE [*continuous*]: . . . that if you compare Dave to the majority of—
I mean, Jesus, I can't believe I'm suddenly standing here defending
Dave.

DON: I *admire* Dave.

DOCTOR [*to* DON]: Let us go downstairs.

DON [*ignoring the* DOCTOR]: We're the ones owe *you and Dave* the
apology.

DOCTOR: Don?

DON [*contained but pissed*]: Doctor, you are not my *nanny,* so would
you kindly stop hovering and clucking at me like some goddamn
nursemaid *mother hen?*

[NANCY *enters brandishing a small card.* JANE *turns and exits to the
bathroom.*]

NANCY [*to* DON, *coldly*]: Let's just get one thing straight. Just so there's
no misunderstanding about who's *bright* and who *isn't.*

DON [*knowing what is coming*]: Oh *put it away.*

NANCY: I'd like everyone to take a little look at something.

DON: We've all *seen* it.

NANCY: And I specifically direct your attention to the name embossed
in the lower left-hand *corner.*

DON [*wearily*]: We've all seen the *Mensa card,* Nancy. You're a very smart woman, now put it away.

[*The* DOCTOR *exits, unnoticed.* JANE *returns, drying her hair.*]

NANCY: They don't just hand these out on the street corner, all right? It's a *six-hour test! Six hours, with no break* [*without a breath, instantly gracious to* JANE] it has been *so* nice meeting you. We are just *thrilled* having you here [*stage whisper*] *but I think maybe I'm coming down with a little something* [*silently mouths the rest*] *and I'm sure I'll feel a lot better in the morning.*

[*She exits.* JANE *is searching the room, in constant motion.*]

DON: See, what I think is this: I think Dave and I, your fiancé and I—

JANE [*a bit manically*]: Sorry. Can we not use that word, okay? The word "fiancé"?

DON: You looking for something?

JANE: A blue backpack. I mean, yes, okay, sure, if you're stuck in some *country* in the middle of an actual *jungle* and someone goes down, *literally* down on one knee and asks you this particular question, well, what are you supposed to do? Say *no*?

DON [*pointing*]: What's that over there?

JANE: I mean, Dave is very sweet— [*Finding the backpack*] Thank you. But the *judgment,* you know? What, because I don't choose to be out there wielding a *hammer* in the middle of some fucking *typhoon*?

[*She struggles with the zipper.*]

DON: What's that, stuck?

JANE [*sourly*]: *Fiancé.* Never mind that I happen to have flown halfway around the world just to . . . and, incidentally, does he ever stop and think about the kind of *paycheck* I'm walking away from? No. The kind of *money* they're willing to pay you in Hollywood to appear in that kind of— [*Re: the zipper*] God, this thing is like—

DON [*re: the zipper*]: Maybe don't pull.

JANE: But still, my level of commitment is somehow *insufficient*? As my agents are practically foaming at the mouth eight thousand miles away, and furthermore, it's called *fibromyalgia*, Dave. Okay? It's a *disease.* So if for *one night,* I happen to prefer to sleep on an actual *mattress* instead of some— *Okay, can someone please explain the concept behind this fucking zipper!!??*

[*She hurls the backpack across the room, then slumps down with her head in her hands as* AUNTIE MIMI *appears at the door, phone pressed to her ear.*]

AUNTIE MIMI [*into phone*]: Je vais lui demander. Attendez, s'il vous plaît. [*Tr: I will ask her. Wait please.*]

[*to* JANE] Miz Adams, would you please tell me what color shirt your fiancé was wearing?

JANE [*to* DON]: I don't know what she means.

AUNTIE MIMI: The color of the shirt, please.

DON: Whose shirt, you mean *Dave's* shirt?

JANE [*to* DON]: It was a blue shirt.

AUNTIE MIMI [*into phone*]: Un polo bleu. Oui, d'accord. [*To* JANE] Do not leave, please.

[AUNTIE MIMI *exits. Pause.* DON *slowly picks* JANE's *backpack up, returns it to her. He unzips it with no effort.*]

70

DON: Gotta line the teeth up.

JANE: Thanks.

DON: Kinda tricky.

JANE: Thank you very much.

DON [*gently*]: Tell you the truth. Truth is I think Dave and I probably have more in common than you might— See, Dave— Well, Dave's young, Dave's an optimist. Little idealistic, maybe . . . [*cont'd*]

JANE [*gently overlapping*]: Sorry, I really do have to go.

DON [*continuous*]: . . . but I know what he thinks. Person like Dave. You too, maybe. You look at me, think to yourself, here's this old guy, guy who's only out for himself, guy who's all about *the bottom line*, and that's not what I'm all about.

JANE: Well, I can't speak for Dave—

DON: I'm just a person. Person with feelings.

JANE: I understand that.

DON: And I certainly don't think they *spit* at me, do they, these kids? Never seen *that*. Spit on my car?

JANE: He shouldn't have said that.

DON: 'Cause I tell ya, you get to be my age and all you do every single day is, you sit around asking yourself whether or not you've really made a . . . made some kinda positive— Not to dwell on myself, but like you. Same as you. Here you were, you had this job, wasn't rewarding somehow, something missing from your life, and so you went and *changed* it. And I can't tell ya how much I relate to that. What you and Dave are doing down there. Making a difference in these people's lives. Fundamental human . . . responsibility, and that's the point I'm trying to make: Maybe it's giving people jobs, maybe it's giving them an education, like you and

Dave, but otherwise what does it amount to in the end of all? If you can't get outa bed in the morning and look in the mirror and say to yourself—

JANE [*dismissively*]: I don't know. I don't know, I just saw these faces in the paper, you know? Having my coffee one morning and these little faces staring up at me in the paper. These little faces the same color as my coffee and those *eyes,* you know, staring up at the camera, and beneath the picture where it says how for less than a dollar a day, for less than the price of a cup of coffee and believe me, I am by *no* stretch of the imagination a religious person, not even *remotely,* so forgive the grandiosity but I just wanted to *know* that it was possible for someone like me— And I swear to you, from the very first moment I set foot here— Well, I mean, not counting the two weeks of nonstop *diarrhea,* because the *people,* you know? With, with, with— I mean, yes, let's face it, there's the corruption and the homophobia and the genital mutilation, but when I met the *children*—or, at least those that aren't openly *hostile*— It's just, all of a sudden I'm *standing* there, right? And I'm looking around at everything, you know, at this tiny little *classroom,* and the chalkboard, and Patrice and *Dave,* and I just, I don't know, *still,* this *one thought* kept going through my head.

[*Small pause.*]

DON: *Get me the hell outa this shithole.*

JANE [*trying not to laugh, and failing*]: No no no no no no. It's just that no one mentions all the *dirt* and the *garbage* and these people just [*lowering voice*] dropping their pants and *taking a shit right out in the middle of the*—?

DON: And the *heat*?!

JANE: Oh my *god.* You hear *tropical* and you think, oh, *that'll be good for my skin.*

DON: Or the *smell.*

JANE: I— The what?

DON: You know the smell I'm talking about.

JANE: Ohh. Let's not say that.

DON: But you *know.*

JANE: But let's not say it.

DON: But you're *thinking* it.

JANE: Maybe occasionally I think it.

DON: *Occasionally?* [cont'd]

JANE [*overlapping*]: I know, but if you take into consideration . . .
    [*cont'd*]

DON [*continuous, overlapping*]: Spend about half the time holding my
    breath.

JANE [*continuous*]: . . . the, uh, you know, various economic factors—

DON: You gonna say it, or me?

JANE [*laughing*]: *Okay, the B.O.!!! Now I've said it.*

DON: *God almighty!*

JANE: The *incredibly pungent B.O.!!!*

DON: *Somebody airlift these folks a year's supply of Arrid Extra Dry
    and charge it to me!!*

JANE: I know. We're both going to hell, but I know.

[*Beat.*]

    And what, now I'm supposed to go live in some *shed*? I said Dave,
    please, you know, people have *limits.*

DON: So stay.

JANE: I can't.

DON: Sure you can.

JANE: I have to go.

DON: Ah, c'mon.

JANE: I really do.

DON: Just the one night.

JANE: No no. Two more minutes, then I'll definitely go.

[*Low thunder. Neither of them move.*]

Although. Do you mind if I ask? Um, what was it, exactly, that . . . happened . . . to Father Tom?

DON: Ohhh boy. Yeah, that was a real shame, but, uh— Put it this way. Suffice it to say, a *hacksaw* was involved.

JANE: Huh. Guess I missed that part when I was filling out my application.

[*The audience hears voices approaching.* NANCY *enters, with* AUNTIE MIMI *and* SOLDIER 1.]

NANCY [*visibly nervous*]: Don?

AUNTIE MIMI [*to* JANE]: Miz Adams, you are positive when you say that Father Dave's shirt was blue?

JANE [*to* DON]: She saw his shirt.

AUNTIE MIMI: And did you observe in what direction he was walking?

JANE: Ummm, downhill, so . . . west?

AUNTIE MIMI: And did you see him get into a car?

JANE: No. I mean, it was raining too hard to—

AUNTIE MIMI: Can you think of any reason that he would get into a car?

JANE: I— For a *ride*?

AUNTIE MIMI: Does he make a practice of getting into the cars of strangers?

DON: Mimi, just tell us what the hell's going on.

AUNTIE MIMI [*to* SOLDIER 1]: Vous-êtes sûr de ce que vous-avez vu? [*Tr: You're sure of what you saw?*]

SOLDIER 1: Ouais. [*Tr: Yeah.*]

AUNTIE MIMI: Vous-êtes sûr que c'etait lui? [*Tr: You're sure that it was him?*]

SOLDIER 1: Ouais.

[AUNTIE MIMI *indicates for* SOLDIER 1 *to step forward. At her gesture, he speaks.*]

[*awkwardly, to* DON *and* JANE] I think mebbe dey is problem.

[*Lights fade onstage.*]

ACT 2

[*In the darkness, the sound of a ringing phone, as heard from the caller's earpiece. Lights rise on* NANCY *and* JANE. *It is now very late. Frogs chirp outside. On the other side of the room, the* DOCTOR *sleeps soundly in a chair, his glasses perched atop his head.* JANE *has her cell phone pressed to her ear. She has changed out of the wet dress—which now hangs from the bathroom door—and into sweatpants and a shirt, also provided, the audience can assume, by* NANCY. NANCY *has changed into nighttime clothing as well. Eventually,* JANE *pushes a button to end the call.*]

NANCY: No?

JANE: No.

NANCY: Do you think he turned it off?

JANE: No.

NANCY: Do people keep asking that?

JANE: Yeah.

NANCY: And you don't think he would.

JANE: No.

NANCY: I turn mine off sometimes.

JANE: Mmm.

NANCY: If I don't feel like talking.

[*Beat.*]

Which apparently is something that could stand to happen a little more often as far as some people are concerned.

JANE: Really?

NANCY: Don.

JANE: Ah.

NANCY: Got on my case about it.

[*Beat.*]

And I suppose there could be a measure of truth to what he says.

[*Pause.*]

You'd rather be alone.

JANE: No.

NANCY: You would.

JANE: No.

NANCY: It's okay.

JANE: I wouldn't.

NANCY: You can tell me if you want me to go.

JANE: No, stay.

NANCY: I was just worried about you sitting here alone.

JANE: Thanks.

NANCY: But you say the word and I will just absolutely go.

JANE: Okay.

[*Pause. From across the room, the* DOCTOR *snores very loudly.* JANE *starts to dial her cell phone, and when* NANCY *speaks,* JANE *stops.*]

NANCY: But see, I get self-conscious when . . . [*seeing* JANE *stop*] Oh no no no no, go ahead and call.

JANE: It's okay.

NANCY: Did I stop you? Don't let me stop you.

JANE: Either he'll call back or— So, you get self-conscious.

NANCY: Well, *now,* especially. Now that he's *made* me.

JANE: Who?

NANCY: Don. So, I'm supposed to, what? Just *keep everything to my-self?* And particularly now, right? When we happen to be living in a time period, am I right, when people could maybe be a little sympathetic?

JANE: Which time period?

NANCY: Since 9-11.

JANE: Oh right.

NANCY: *Particularly* now.

JANE: Did you, I mean . . . *lose* someone?

NANCY: Well, my brother.

JANE: Oh, god.

NANCY: No, *he* lost someone.

JANE: Ohhh. Someone . . . close?

NANCY: Well, his wife—

JANE: Oh god.

NANCY: No, she has a *sister*.

JANE: Ah.

NANCY: Whose best friend from high school's cousin was, yes, you know. *Splat.*

JANE: Right.

NANCY: And things like that are just extremely hard for me to recover from.

JANE: No. I mean, yeah. I think you're— Yeah.

NANCY: So if by chance some of us should commit the *unforgivable crime* of being slightly emotional at this moment in human— And Ashlee always goes *here comes Niagara Falls Nancy*. That girl can be a cold hearted little— You don't have children?

JANE: No.

NANCY [*sympathetically*]: And that is *totally fine*. You should *not* regret that. Because trust me, if you ever want a good swift dose of— Do you have time for a story?

JANE: I— I— I—

NANCY: I'll leave you alone.

JANE: No.

NANCY: Look at me proving Don's point for him.

JANE: But if you're—? If you need to—?

NANCY: Oh, I don't sleep. I never sleep. It's weird. Ever. Isn't that weird?

JANE: That is weird.

NANCY: But you're worried.

JANE: I'm okay.

NANCY: You're scrunching up your forehead.

JANE: Sorry.

NANCY: But you left him a message, right?

JANE: Several, yeah.

NANCY: Then I'm sure he's *fine.*

JANE: And I'm fine too, but uhh . . . I mean, either way.

[*Pause. The* DOCTOR *mutters something unintelligible in French, shifts.*]

NANCY: Well, just the one story, then. So. You know how kids can be. Well, maybe you don't, but they always think their parents are so totally *appalling* anyway, and Ashlee was having a little sleep-over—this is back during junior high school—you know, a slumber party with her little girlfriends, and lemme tell you, if there is one thing that they will *never,* I mean *ever* forgive it's if Mom or Dad should ever entertain a single [*lowering voice*] *sexual* thought in their heads, I mean *how revolting,* never mind that's how her little ass came into existence. Anyway, the fact of the matter is that, okay *yes.* I do *happen* to be one of those women who owns a [*out of the corner of her mouth*] d-i-l-d-o, okay? I confess. You know, *lock me up.* As if that's *sooooo* unusual. And so her girlfriends are there having their little slumber party and well, okay, remember I told you about our dog Shee-shee? [*In baby voice*] *Wiff her liddle widdle fuzzy faish?* [*Normally*] Well, Shee-shee . . . how do I . . . ? Uhhh . . . you know how some dogs just have kind of a thing about *chewing*? [*Laughing*] Oh, my god. Ashlee goes *she was chewing on your big purple dildo, Mom!! Right in front of all my friends!! Now everyone at school is going to be talking about the disgusting giant purple rubber thing you like stick up your—* Etcetera, and I say *all right,* Ashlee. Calm down and take the dog for a walk, and she says *are you crazy?!! When she takes a poop she's going to poop out big purple chunks of your dil—* [*Without stopping, seeing* JANE's *face*] —okay, maybe this is inappropriate.

JANE: Um—

NANCY: I can see the look on your face.

JANE: I don't know.

NANCY [*factually*]: See what I do? How I alienate people? How I try to be all ingratiating and amusing and consequently people *avoid* me, which is so ironic since I was just trying to get them to like me in the first place.

JANE: Maybe you're exaggerating.

NANCY: *Oh* no. People *despise* me. No, they do. They really do. I don't know why.

[*She laughs.*]

I despise *myself*!

[JANE's *cell phone rings.*]

[*Simply*] Did you ever try to kill yourself? I once tried to kill myself.

JANE [to NANCY]: Just a second. [Answering phone] Hello?

NANCY: Is it him? Is that him?

JANE [into phone]: Oui, Patrice, c'est moi. [Tr: Yes, Patrice, it's me.]

[DON and AUNTIE MIMI, in the middle of a quiet disagreement, enter.]

DON: . . . but if that is the case, then in that event, it would behoove us— [To JANE] Is that him? [As JANE shakes her head, back to AUNTIE MIMI] —behoove all of us, to have some strategy.

AUNTIE MIMI: But this is precisely his function, Don, as your representative.

DON: No, now let's not go waking people up in the middle of the night.

JANE [into phone]: No, Patrice? No, derrière la maison. [Tr: Behind the house.] C'est une— Shit. [To the room] How do I say the word shed?

AUNTIE MIMI [to DON]: What does she mean, shed?

JANE: Like, a shed. Like, you know, like a—

AUNTIE MIMI [to JANE]: What about a shed?

JANE: Not a lean-to, more like a . . . enclosed—

DON [to AUNTIE MIMI]: No use dragging people into something until we're sure of what it is we're dealing with.

JANE [into phone]: Un petit structure? Oui. D'accord. Merci, Patrice. [Tr: A little building? Yes. Okay. Thank you, Patrice.]

[She hangs up.]

AUNTIE MIMI: But the point at which we have this assurance? That is the point at which it will be too late.

JANE: Sorry. Can we maybe not get ahead of ourselves?

DON: Right. She's right.

JANE: We only know one or two things. And for the purposes of my sanity—

AUNTIE MIMI: We know about the car.

JANE: *Suspect* about the car.

AUNTIE MIMI: And now we know about the phone.

JANE: No. All we know is, I left a message.

AUNTIE MIMI: You called, you left a message.

JANE: Several.

AUNTIE MIMI: And then no answer. Meaning one of two things. Either *he* turned it off after your message . . .

DON: Not necessarily.

AUNTIE MIMI: Or, someone else, and we cannot say who, turned it off *for* him.

JANE: Well, I'm sorry, but I consider that a *leap*.

AUNTIE MIMI [*conciliating*]: I understand. You hope for that. We all hope for that.

JANE: Well, I know Dave, and you don't.

AUNTIE MIMI: How long have you known him?

JANE: What diff— I don't know. Two months? Long *enough*.

AUNTIE MIMI: Well, I have known him a good deal longer.

JANE: And I think what Dave would say, were he here to say it . . .
[*cont'd*]

AUNTIE MIMI [*overlapping*]: Which he is not.

JANE [*continuous*]: . . . is that some of us seem *very* eager to make this leap into *paranoia*.

AUNTIE MIMI: Is that what you think?

DON: Mimi, the only thing that matters—

AUNTIE MIMI [*to* JANE]: You think it is paranoia?

JANE: Why does Dave need permission to get into someone's *car*?

[*The* DOCTOR *snores.*]

DON: The only thing that matters here—

JANE [*finally snapping, re: the* DOCTOR]: God, can somebody *poke* him or something?

AUNTIE MIMI: Excuse me, Don. [*To* JANE] Wait here, please.

[AUNTIE MIMI *exits. Pause.* DON *looks at his watch, listens to see if it is ticking.*]

DON [*re: his watch*]: Jesus, what has become of the *Swiss*? [*To* NANCY] Time you got?

[NANCY *pointedly does not answer.*]

[*To* JANE, *re:* NANCY] What's the deal with her?

JANE: She's, uhhh . . . it's hard to—

NANCY: I was insulted by what you said to me, Don. No, I was, but after thinking about it, I realize that you were simply trying to tell me something for my own good, something about the way I am inevitably perceived by the world . . . [*cont'd*]

DON [*quietly, overlapping*]: Oh boy.

NANCY [*continuous*]: . . . which, I suppose, was actually *cathartic,* in a way, to hear it out loud, hear what everyone has been thinking all along, that there is something inherently loathsome about me as a person, which I now must make it a part of my journey to accept.

DON [*to* JANE]: You got the time?

JANE [*looking at her watch*]: Quarter past three.

DON: So. Six hours since he left. Give or take.

JANE: You know, seriously, why don't the two of you go to bed?

DON: No no. Let's get this straightened out.

NANCY: Am I *insensitive?* I don't think so. I think I'm *overly* sensitive. But I *suppose* that could be it.

DON [*calmly*]: Could be *what?*

NANCY: Why so many people detest me.

DON: Honey? Nobody understands what it is you're *talking* about.

[AUNTIE MIMI *returns with* SOLDIER 1, *who eats an orange as he speaks.* AUNTIE MIMI *snaps her fingers at* SOLDIER 1.]

AUNTIE MIMI: Voilà. Allez-y, s'il vous plaît. Expliquez-le à cette femme. [*Tr: Here. Go ahead, please. Explain it to this woman.*]

SOLDIER 1: Uhhh . . . nous venions du marché en voiture. Il pleuvait. Nous avons vu cette voiture. [*Tr: We were driving here from the market. It was raining. We saw this car.*]

AUNTIE MIMI [*to* DON]: It was raining. They saw the car. [*To* SOLDIER 1] Quel type de voiture? [*Tr: What type of car?*]

SOLDIER 1: Toyota camionnette. Bleu-foncée. [*Tr: A small Toyota pickup. Dark blue.*]

AUNTIE MIMI: A small blue truck.

SOLDIER 1 [*to* JANE]: Nous avons vu la voiture venir de la direction opposée, avec quelques hommes à l'arrière. [*Tr: We saw the car coming from the other direction, with some men in the back.*]

DON [*to* AUNTIE MIMI]: Translate.

JANE [*to* DON]: They passed a car, uh . . . going the opposite way.

SOLDIER 1: Et quand nous les avons croisés, j'ai regardé dans le miroir. Il y avait trois hommes, et un blanc. [*Tr: And as we passed, I looked in the mirror. There were three men, and one white man.*]

AUNTIE MIMI: In the back, four men. One, a white man.

SOLDIER 1: Et j'ai vu . . . que c'est Fada Dave. [*Tr: And I saw . . . that it was Father Dave.*]

DON: They *both* saw Dave?

AUNTIE MIMI: L'avez-vous vu tous les deux? [*Tr: Did both of you see him?*]

SOLDIER 1: Ouais, bien sûr. [*Tr: Yeah, sure.*]

AUNTIE MIMI [*to* SOLDIER 1]: Et où avez-vous vu ces camionnettes? [*Tr: And where have you seen these trucks?*]

SOLDIER 1: Je les ai vues conduites par des gens du PPEG. [*Tr: I have seen them driven by some of the PPEG.*]

AUNTIE MIMI [*pointedly, to* JANE]: *A car like those of the PPEG.*

JANE: Okay. And that proves what?

[AUNTIE MIMI *snaps her fingers at* SOLDIER 1.]

AUNTIE MIMI: Bon. Allez-y. [*Tr: Fine. Go.*]

[SOLDIER 1 *exits.*]

JANE: As far as I can tell, it proves nothing.

AUNTIE MIMI: Then call to make sure. Ah, that is right. He does not answer.

JANE: Well, *possibly* he does not *choose* to answer due to the fact that we were treating him like shit.

DON: No reason you gotta stick around, Mimi.

AUNTIE MIMI: I am going nowhere.

JANE [*to* AUNTIE MIMI]: Listen. People do things for specific reasons. People have *motivations*.

AUNTIE MIMI: In a *television program*, yes. But we happen to live in the *natural* world.

[DON *starts to rub his left arm.*]

In nature there is the crocodile, and the crocodile will kill for sport. Now, we could sit all day, ask what *motivates* the crocodile, and when we are done, it will still try to bite us. So what to do? Try to understand the creature? No. We bind the jaws so it can no longer bite.

[*A phone rings.* AUNTIE MIMI *and* JANE *grab their cell phones as* NANCY *tugs at* DON's *sleeve.*]

JANE:	AUNTIE MIMI:
Hello? Hell— [*Realizing it was*	Allô? Oui? Oui, d'accord.
AUNTIE MIMI's *phone*] Oh.	[*Tr: Hello? Yes? Yes, okay.*]

NANCY [*to* DON]: Why were you rubbing your arm?

AUNTIE MIMI: Allez-y. Je vous écoute. [*Tr: Go ahead. I am listening.*]

NANCY: Is it hurting?

DON: I wasn't rubbing it.

NANCY: You had your hand like this.

DON: Scratching, maybe.

NANCY: Was it tingling?

DON: Itching, I guess.

NANCY: Itching? Or tingling?

DON: I don't remember *doing* it.

AUNTIE MIMI: Oui, appelez-moi encore dans quinze minutes. [*Tr: Yes, call me again in fifteen minutes.*]

[*She hangs up.*]

JANE [*to* AUNTIE MIMI]: Let me tell you something I find to be offensive. In my country we don't generally equate people with *animals.*

AUNTIE MIMI: Would you like to know what *I* find offensive? I find *decapitation* to be offensive.

NANCY [*fingers in her ears, closing her eyes*]: Hmm-mm-mmm. No no no no no.

[*She hums a tune to herself.*]

AUNTIE MIMI: Cutting off a man's *head,* placing the severed head in a plastic bag, and leaving it to be discovered. *That* I find offensive.

JANE: *Jesus, maybe his battery's dead! Did that thought occur to anyone?*

AUNTIE MIMI: *And* it is offensive to me that an *actress* from *Southern California . . .* [*cont'd*]

JANE [*overlapping, dialing her phone*]: You know what? We *get it.* You had a *bad time* in California.

AUNTIE MIMI [*continuous*]: . . . a person who could have died when her residence was nearly *burned to the ground yesterday* would speak to me in such an impudent and insulting manner . . . [*cont'd*]

DON [*overlapping*]: Mimi. We're sorry.

AUNTIE MIMI [*continuous*]: . . . while I am doing my utmost to help her.

[JANE *puts the phone to her ear.*]

JANE [*holding up a finger to* DON]: Wait wait wait. It's picking up. It's— [*Into phone*] Okay, um, Dave? Okay, look, I don't know whether or not you're getting these? [*cont'd*]

[AUNTIE MIMI *exits, exasperated.*]

But people are kind of starting to freak out around here, so even if you're . . . mad or, whatever, just . . . just do me a favor and call back, okay? It's important. All right?

[*She hangs up.* NANCY *still hums, fingers in ears, eyes closed.* JANE *touches* NANCY's *leg.*]

NANCY [*opening her eyes, taking fingers out of ears*]: Oh.

[DON *stands. The* DOCTOR *snores.* DON *gives the* DOCTOR *a shake.*]

DON: Doctor?

DOCTOR [*with a start*]: Qu'y a-t-il? Je suis éveillé. [*Tr: What is it? I am awake.*]

DON: Getting a little noisy, there.

DOCTOR [*to the bathroom door*]: I was not asleep, you know. I was closing my eyes, that is all.

DON [*to* JANE *and* NANCY]: 'Scuse me a second.

[DON *exits into the bathroom.* JANE'*s wristwatch beeps.*]

JANE: Whoops.

[*She reaches in a pocket for her bottle of pills.*]

NANCY [*to* JANE]: So. What I did was, I closed all the garage doors and I turned on the ignition, then I rolled down all the windows so the fumes could circulate, and then I pulled that little handle to recline the seat—

JANE: Sorry. What are we—?

NANCY: The time I tried to— You know. When I decided to . . . "____" myself?

JANE: Right.

NANCY: And I was lying there waiting, and then I started to realize that if you have a four-car garage, it really does take a *long* time to fill the whole thing up with carbon monoxide. But you would never do anything like that.

JANE [*swallowing pills*]: Uhh, hard to say.

NANCY: Noooo. People love you. [*Off of* JANE'*s look*] Oh, of *course* they do. You're on *TV.* [*Ruefully*] You can't tell Don has a little thing for you?

JANE: For—? *Noooooo.*

NANCY: Oh, like I care.

JANE: I think you're— No.

NANCY: I'm not going to make a big thing about it.

JANE: I think you're wrong.

NANCY: Uhh, I *know* him.

JANE: I'm *sure* you're wrong.

NANCY: Doesn't take a *genius.*

JANE: Seriously.

NANCY: All right.

JANE: That's just not true.

NANCY: If you say so.

JANE: I do say so.

[*Pause.*]

NANCY [*laughing*]: Funny though, I can never figure out when it was he stopped feeling that way about *me.*

JANE: Nancy.

NANCY [*sensing* DON's *return*]: Sh-sh-sh.

[DON *opens the bathroom door, drying his face with a towel.*]

What's the matter?

DON: Who're you talking to, me?

NANCY: Are you warm?

DON: I'm fine.

NANCY: Well, you don't look fine.

DON [*to* JANE]: How you holdin' up?

JANE: Me too. Fine.

DON: How's the, uhhh . . . [*indicates neck and shoulders*]

JANE: Much better.

DON [*re: the pills*]: Stuff seem to be working for you?

JANE: Whatever it is. *Crack,* for all I care.

DON: Ours is not to question why.

JANE: No, are you kidding? I'm grateful. [*Over her shoulder to the* DOCTOR] *Thank you.*

NANCY [*to the* DOCTOR]: Doctor, does Don look fine to you?

[*The* DOCTOR *is preparing to light another joint.*]

DOCTOR: I was not sleeping, you know.

DON [*to the* DOCTOR]: Might be time you got yourself to bed.

NANCY: I think he should stay.

DON: I just told you, I'm *fine.*

NANCY: Well, *I'd* prefer that he stayed.

DON: Nance?

NANCY: Oh, so I happen to notice that you have pain in your arm and I'm not allowed to be *concerned*?

DON: I appreciate the concern, but—

NANCY: Then why are you getting angry?

DOCTOR [*re: the joint*]: Will this be a problem for anyone?

DON [*to* NANCY]: Honey, I'm just asking if it might be possible, when we're in the middle of a situation like this, couldn't we all just maybe try to . . . to . . . to—

JANE: Transcend.

DON: Right, *to rise above* our own petty little . . . [*cont'd*]

NANCY [*quietly overlapping*]: I know what the word "transcend" means.

DON [*continuous*]: . . . insignificant differences, I mean, gee whiz, can't we all, at the very least . . . [*cont'd*]

JANE [*overlapping, to* DON]: Nancy's been very helpful. No, she has.

DON [*continuous*]: . . . try and take some of the focus off of *ourselves* for the time being?

NANCY: I think we both know where your focus is.

DON [*to* JANE]: What's that supposed to mean?

NANCY: Oh, I think you know.

JANE: Nancy.

NANCY: And I'd be interested to know what you imagine I've been *doing* for the past five and a half hours. Not to mention your entire *birthday,* but does anyone ever say *thank you, Nancy?*

DON [*to* NANCY]: I'm sorry. I should've thanked you.

DOCTOR [*with a big yawn*]: Ohhhh, it is so interesting the way that people think. Because you know, it is so many centuries that people have been coming to this country. [*cont'd*]

DON [*overlapping*]: Ahh, brother.

DOCTOR [*continuous*]: But what is interesting about the *Americans* is that they are convinced that they are very *different.* Do you see? You always say to us, no no no, we are not like the Belgians or the French or the English. [*cont'd*]

DON [*overlapping, to* JANE]: Good thing we woke him up.

DOCTOR [*continuous*]: *We* don't want to *prosper.* No, the Americans, you see, they must always believe they have come to this country *for the good of the world.* [*cont'd*]

DON: Doctor?

DOCTOR [*continuous*]: As if we should say to them *thank you. Thank you America.* But we never mention that this is the same thing people have been promising to us for the past five hundred years.

DON: Sorry, you know what? Really not the time or place.

DOCTOR [*innocently*]: I am joining the conversation.

DON: No you're not.

DOCTOR: It is a *private* conversation?

DON: You're being *critical.* And I don't have a problem with criticism at the proper *time.*

NANCY: Maybe just point when you want us to speak, Don.

JANE [*to* DON]: But I think what he's saying, if I may?

DON [*remaining above it all*]: No no, I know what he's saying. Same negative little pessimistic opinion of the world he's always pontificating about and it just gets a little tiresome after a while, is all.

JANE: But I think he's asking whether there might be an element of hypocrisy if we, you know, if we—

DOCTOR: Don, I am *sympathetic* to Americans.

DON: Oh, think I'm gonna cry.

DOCTOR: It is *sad* to me that you cannot *enjoy* all your prosperity. That your business will prosper. [*Indicating* JANE] That this woman, she will be congratulated for her good deeds and then *she* will prosper. And still—

DON: Lemme tell you something.

JANE [*to the* DOCTOR]: Wait a second. You think I wouldn't *rather*—? That if it wasn't for these *children*, children who happen to be *uneducated*, okay? Happen to be *suffering*—?

DON [*to* JANE]: 'Scuse me. [*To the* DOCTOR] And you know something else? I don't exactly see *you* living hand to mouth. If prosperity is such a terrible thing.

DOCTOR: Who said this?

DON: You're trying to tell me these people here, living in some miserable dirt-floor shack with nothing but a hole in the ground to shit in, you think these people don't *want* to better their lives, don't want to *prosper*? How d'you think an emerging economy is *supposed* to function, *dummy*?

DOCTOR [*to* JANE]: Ah, listen to what he calls me.

DON: Tell you what. Soon as we find Dave. You talk to Dave. Dave reads the Bible. *Bible* isn't telling people to be *poor*. Bible's *telling* you to prosper. That's what the Bible *wants* you to do. Says to *prosper*. To live long and, and, and, and, and . . . [*realizing his mistake*] wait a second.

[NANCY *and the* DOCTOR *laugh.*]

[*To the* DOCTOR] Yeah, that's right. Go ahead and snicker, ya little prick. [*To others*] Sits around on his ass all day, that's the problem with half the people in this country.

JANE: Wait. Whoa. Let's not stoop to, you know—

DON: Sits there making cracks at the expense of a guest here in my home, woman's made all sorts of sacrifices just so she could come to do these poor people here in your country a little bit of *good*.

DOCTOR [to JANE]: Oh, could you find no poor people in *your* country?

DON: *Oh, give it a rest.*

[AUNTIE MIMI *enters, holding cell phone.*]

AUNTIE MIMI [*holding out phone for* DON *to take*]: Don? Speak to him, please.

DON [*grumbling*]: Listening to his bullshit day in and day out just because he happens to be from this part of the world—yeah, *so what?* I'm supposed to get down on my knees every time he issues one of his little *pronouncements?* [*Muttering*] Fucking infuriating.

AUNTIE MIMI: He is waiting, Don.

DON [*to the* DOCTOR]: If you'd even done *half* of what this woman's done for your own people.

DOCTOR: They cannot *pay* me, Don. If you want me to work for them, stop paying me to work for *you.*

DON [*to* NANCY]: First good idea he's had in a long time.

DOCTOR: I see, am I being fired?

DON: Don't need him trailing me everywhere I go, and I'm sure as hell not paying him to get *stoned* twenty-four hours a day.

DOCTOR: If I am fired, I will go back to sleep.

NANCY: Stay right there.

DON [*to the* DOCTOR]: Tell you what, bud. Read up on a little history.

[AUNTIE MIMI *snaps her fingers.*]

AUNTIE MIMI: *Don.*

DOCTOR: Which part of history?

DON [*taking phone*]: Hello?

DOCTOR [*re:* AUNTIE MIMI]: The part where *her* ancestors sold *my* ancestors to *your* ancestors?

DON [*into phone*]: Ah hell, Howard. I told Mimi not to get you outa bed.

[JANE's *cell phone rings.*]

NANCY: *It's him. I bet that's him. Shhhh!!!*

JANE [*struggling with phone*]: *Shit*— Wait wait wait wait wait. [*Into phone*] Hello?

DON [*to* JANE]: What happened? Is that Dave?

JANE [*putting a finger in her other ear*]: Wait. Sorry, I can't— Dave?

DON [*into phone*]: Hang on, Howard. I think we got him.

NANCY: Is he all right? Ask him if he's all right.

DON [*into phone*]: Howard, lemme call you back.

[*He hangs up.*]

JANE: Wait a second, who is this?

AUNTIE MIMI [*to* JANE]: Find out the location. Get the location.

JANE: Well for Christ's sake, look at a *clock* next time. And maybe an atlas.

AUNTIE MIMI: How many are with him? Who is making the call for him?

DON: *If we'd all shut up for a second maybe she could hear the goddamn phone call!!*

JANE [*into phone*]: Jeff, I don't *care* how much they're offering. This is not *about* money, okay? This is about my *life* and I happen to be in the middle of something extremely *serious.*

[*She hangs up. All stare at her.*]

NANCY: Ohmigod. That was your agent. Was that your agent?

[*Noise is heard from outside the door.*]

VOICE FROM OUTSIDE: *Je vous ai déjà dit ce que je veux!! Je veux ma* *chaussure. Donnez-moi ma chaussure!* [*Tr: I already told you what* *I want!! I want my shoe. Give me my shoe!*]

[SOLDIER 1 *and* SOLDIER 2 *enter, dragging a shirtless figure with a* *loose-fitting black hood on his head and his hands tied behind his back.* *One of the* SOLDIERS *also carries* ETIENNE's *filthy backpack, the same* *color as* JANE's.]

HOODED FIGURE:	SOLDIER 2:	AUNTIE MIMI:	DON:
Je vous ai dit de	*Boucle-la,*	Ah, merde alors!	*No no no*
me lâcher le	*casse-cul!!*	Que se passe-	*no!* Not in
bras!! [*Tr: I told*	[*Tr: Shut up,*	t-il? [*Tr: Oh,*	here! Not
you to let go	*you pain in*	*shit! What's*	in this
of my arm!!]	*the ass!!*]	*going on?*]	room!

SOLDIER 1 [*to* AUNTIE MIMI]: Nous l'avons trouvé dehors. Il montait sur le mur. [*Tr: We found him outside. He was climbing over the* *wall.*]

AUNTIE MIMI: Je ne m'inquiète pas! Pourquoi devez-vous l'apporter ici? Enlevez-le. [*Tr: I don't care! Why must you bring him in here?* *Take him away.*]

HOODED FIGURE: *You go break mai arm, you stoopid soja muthfucka!*

[SOLDIER 2 *raises the butt of his rifle and smacks the* HOODED FIGURE *in the back, sending him to the ground. All shout in response, "Whoa!"* *"Hey!" "Easy now!" etc.*]

JANE [to DON]: *Would you tell them to stop it! For Christ's sake, what is wrong with you people!!?*

AUNTIE MIMI: Silence, please.

JANE: Don't you tell me to be *silent.*

DON: Whoa *whoa*!! Slow down half a second!

SOLDIER 1 [*to* AUNTIE MIMI]: Il dit qu'il recherche une chaussure. [*Tr: He says he's looking for a shoe.*]

AUNTIE MIMI [*to* DON]: This person was found climbing over your wall.

DON: What did he— Something about a *shoe*?

AUNTIE MIMI: He says you have his missing shoe.

DOCTOR: Maybe it is Cinderella.

[AUNTIE MIMI *snaps her fingers at* SOLDIER 1 *and* SOLDIER 2.]

AUNTIE MIMI: Allez-y. Mettez-le sur la chaise. [*Tr: Go ahead. Put him in the chair.*]

[*They do so.*]

JANE: How is he even supposed to *breathe*? [*To* DON] Would you ask them to stop this, please?

SOLDIER 2: C'est le garçon qui était ici la plus tôt aujourd'hui. [*Tr: It is the boy who was here earlier today.*]

AUNTIE MIMI: Ahh, yes, I see.

JANE: It's *who*? What did he say?

AUNTIE MIMI [*to* SOLDIER 1 *and* SOLDIER 2, *re: the hood*]: Enlevez-le. [*Tr: Take it off.*]

[SOLDIER 2 *removes the hood. It is, indeed,* ETIENNE. *One of his eyes is swollen shut, and the area below his nose is caked with dried blood.*]

JANE: Oh my god. Oh, you *sick*—

AUNTIE MIMI: Miz Adams?

JANE: You *sadistic*— This is a *child*, you morons.

AUNTIE MIMI: Yes. A *wicked* child that would destroy the place where you live.

JANE: Oh, so that's a *fact*, now? We just accept that as *fact*?

DON [*pulling* JANE *aside*]: Hang on. Hang on. One thing at a time.

JANE [*to* AUNTIE MIMI]: You want me to talk to the press? Because I will be *more* than happy to talk about *this*. And these two [*indicating* SOLDIER 1 *and* SOLDIER 2] will be in some *very* deep shit.

DON [*quietly, to* JANE]: Okay. But let's think a second.

JANE [*quietly*]: What's she going to do, *silence* me?

DON: But what *if*? I'm just saying for the sake of argument. Let's say he *is* the one that did the fire.

JANE: According to *who*?

DON: Going offa what Dave said. Right? And I'm not saying a *connection*— But is it so unreasonable to just ask, if the next thing we know, *Dave* is suddenly—?

JANE: But based on *what*? Based on *nothing*.

DON [*to* JANE]: Okay. Okay. [*To* ETIENNE, *in a kindly manner*] Son? No one's gonna hurt you. Just want to ask you a question and we'd all prefer a straight answer, okay? Just wanna know if you're the one set that fire last night.

ETIENNE [*laughing*]: Looka di biznessman. Mebbe I say if we do bizness, you an' mi, o?

AUNTIE MIMI: Answer the man.

ETIENNE: No no no. I sabi di bizness. He gif for mi, I gif for him. He gif to mi mai Nike Shox, I tell him true.

DON [*to* AUNTIE MIMI]: Give him what?

JANE: His shoe?

DON: I don't have his shoe.

ETIENNE [*indicating the sneaker from earlier by inclining his head*]: Sittin' ryan fronna yua face.

DON [*seeing the sneaker*]: What, *that* shoe? Gimme that.

ETIENNE [*defiantly*]: An' di Sony. Di Sony dey take from mi. Dey *mai* Sony, man.

DON: Let's answer the question first, huh? How 'bout we do that?

ETIENNE: Ahahaha, dey good. [*To* AUNTIE MIMI] See? Dis di bizness. Now we doin' di bizness heyah.

AUNTIE MIMI [*to* ETIENNE]: Answer the man.

ETIENNE: Sima sima, Auntie! [*Tr: Relax, old lady.*]

AUNTIE MIMI: *Ni ima njaabi I ku be tige!!* [*Tr: You'd better answer or you'll get another smack in the face!!*]

DON: All right *all right.* Just tell us the truth, son.

ETIENNE: Whadda fuck *if* I don di faya? Nobodi sabi di *why*? Nobodi care sabi di *why*?

JANE: Dave did not try to— You know Dave didn't do anything to you.

ETIENNE: Yah, mebbe waz makin' up story, yah. 'Cos Fada Dave, he still to be di beeg faggy man, but Fada Dave not for why don di faya. Don di faya for di Nikes.

DON: He what?

JANE: For the *shoes?*

ETIENNE [*indicating* SOLDIER 1 *and* SOLDIER 2]: Dem two sojas standin' rye dere. Who you think? [*Holding up his feet*] Dem sojas say to me, say Etienne. Say you go an' make us di faya when night is come. We gif to you sontin' guud. I say you gif to mi di paira Nike Shox, I make you di faya. So look.

[*He holds up his feet, now with shoes. The* DOCTOR *finds all of this amusing.*]

An' dey wrong *size,* man! Why you think dey fall offa mi? Dey fuck mi ovah.

AUNTIE MIMI: The boy is a liar.

ETIENNE: No no no, *dey* di layah. An' dey *yua* soja boys, Auntie, 'cos dem, dey work for *you.*

JANE [*having heard enough*]: I'm getting dressed.

DON: Calm down a second.

JANE: Well, how am I supposed to know who to believe?

AUNTIE MIMI [*to* SOLDIER 1 *and* SOLDIER 2]: Avez-vous promis de donner des chaussures à ce garçon? [*Tr: Did you promise to give shoes to this boy?*]

SOLDIER 1 [*innocently*]: Non, Madame. Je vous jure. [*Tr: No, ma'am. I swear to you.*]

SOLDIER 2 [*mumbling*]: Je n'ai jamais vu ce garçon avant hier. [*Tr: I never saw this boy before yesterday.*]

AUNTIE MIMI [*to* JANE]: I suggest you believe the word of two men who have sworn their loyalty to this country.

DON: But Mimi, you understand, we're just trying to reckon with how you said a little bit ago that you wouldn't mind seeing Dave *deported.* Or *worse.*

JANE [*laughing bitterly*]: Ohohoho, god.

[JANE *goes into the bathroom.*]

AUNTIE MIMI: Don. Let us think before we speak. Let us remember who our friends are. And I've always counted myself as your friend.

DOCTOR: The best friend money can buy.

AUNTIE MIMI [*hissing at the* DOCTOR]: *Barka! Vous commencez à me rendre fâchée* [Tr: *Shut up. You're really starting to piss me off.*]

DON [*to* ETIENNE, *less friendly now*]: All right, listen up. Not fooling around anymore, you hear me? You can mouth off to these folks all you want, but I'll tell you right now, I don't think you want to mess around with— [*Pointing in* ETIENNE'*s face*] Look here. Need ya to look at me. You looking at me?

ETIENNE: *Stick yua finga somweh else, o!*

[DON *turns around to* AUNTIE MIMI.]

DON [*quietly to* AUNTIE MIMI]: Where's this little asshole live?

[*With* DON'*s back turned,* ETIENNE *spits a big loogie onto his shoulder.* AUNTIE MIMI *slaps* ETIENNE *in the face.*]

NANCY:	AUNTIE MIMI [*to* ETIENNE]:	DON
Uggghh god.	*Ça y est! Tu cherches un autre*	[*turning around*]:
Oh Don.	*oeil au beurre noir, eh? Si tu*	What happened?
	ne veux pas te faire taper	What did he do?
	dessus, fais gaffe!! [Tr: *That's*	
	it! You want another black eye?	
	Unless you want a fight with	
	me, watch out!]	

NANCY: Eww. Eww. Um, give me your jacket.

AUNTIE MIMI [*to* SOLDIER 1 *and* SOLDIER 2 *re: the hood*]: Allez, portez-la. [*Tr: Put it on.*]

[SOLDIER 1 *and* SOLDIER 2 *replace the hood as* NANCY *exits with the jacket.* JANE *returns from the bathroom with her own clothing, dialing her phone.*]

JANE: Okay, *now,* for some reason? I seem to be missing some of my clothes. [*To* DON] Could Nancy have, possibly, or one of your *servants?*

DON: Who're you calling?

JANE: It's just the one—item? It was hanging on the rod. And if you maybe have a flashlight?

[*At that moment, a cell phone in the room begins to ring. Pause. All stop and look around to determine the source.*]

DON: Whose phone is that?

AUNTIE MIMI [*taking hers out*]: It is not mine.

DON [*to* JANE]: Is that you?

JANE: No, I'm *calling.*

DON: Doctor?

DOCTOR: I have no phone.

AUNTIE MIMI [*to* SOLDIER 1 *and* SOLDIER 2]: À qui téléphone sonne? [*Tr: Whose phone is ringing?*]

[SOLDIER 1 *and* SOLDIER 2 *pull out their cell phones. They shake their heads.*]

DON: Wait a second.

[DON *looks at* ETIENNE. AUNTIE MIMI *snaps her fingers and* SOLDIER 2 *frisks him. He unrolls* ETIENNE's *tightly rolled trouser leg and produces a ringing red cell phone, which he hands to* AUNTIE MIMI.]

ETIENNE [*from under the hood*]: If dey fo' mi? I can' come to di phone rye now.

AUNTIE MIMI [*showing the phone to* JANE]: Do you recognize this telephone?

JANE: I— I—

DON: Is Dave's phone red like that?

JANE: I think— I mean, he *has* a red phone.

DON: Is it that style? Did it sorta look like—?

JANE [*scared*]: *I don't know, okay? How am I supposed to tell one phone from any other phone?*

AUNTIE MIMI [*calmly, to* JANE]: Who is it you say you are calling?

JANE: I was trying to call Dave.

AUNTIE MIMI: And on the other end, is the phone ringing?

[JANE *listens.*]

JANE: Yeah?

AUNTIE MIMI: Hang it up, please.

[JANE *hesitates, then hits the button. The ringing stops. All stare at* JANE.]

JANE [*with determination*]: Okay. I'm going to find him.

DON: No one's leaving.

[JANE *grabs her shoes as* NANCY *slowly returns with* DON's *jacket.*]

AUNTIE MIMI: Let her leave.

NANCY [*coolly detached*]: Well now, *this* is interesting.

JANE: And if anyone happens to come across my clothing? If you could conceivably *forward* it to me?

NANCY: I mean, I *hate* to interrupt.

DON: I really don't think it's safe.

JANE [*making for the door*]: Not *safe*? Well obviously, Don. Not very safe for *Dave.*

AUNTIE MIMI [*to* DON]: Ah yes, and fifteen minutes ago she calls me *paranoid.*

DON: I don't want you to leave.

JANE: Well, thank you. You've been very kind, but what, I'm supposed to just *sit* here?

NANCY: Oh, Don?

DON: *What? For Christ's sake, what?*

NANCY [*calmly factual*]: Well, I don't know, I was just curious as to whom this might belong and how it might have found its way into the pocket of your jacket?

[*She holds up what is clearly a pair of panties. Pause.* JANE *stares at* DON. *The* DOCTOR *and* SOLDIER 1 *and* SOLDIER 2 *begin to laugh.*]

I mean, I'm sure there's a reasonable explanation.

DON: I don't know what you're— [*Turning to* JANE] What, are those yours?

[JANE *goes to* NANCY *to collect her things as* AUNTIE MIMI *approaches* ETIENNE. *The two conversations overlap.*]

AUNTIE MIMI [*to* ETIENNE]:
Comment avez-vous obtenu ce téléphone? [*Tr: How did you get this phone?*]

ETIENNE [*from under the hood*]:
I find it.

AUNTIE MIMI:
Et où l'avez-vous trouvé exactement? [*Tr: And where exactly did you find it?*]

ETIENNE:
I find it here in dis room.

AUNTIE MIMI:
Vous pensez que nous vous croyons? [*Tr: You think that we believe you?*]

ETIENNE:
Auntie, Auntie. I tell you true.

AUNTIE MIMI:
Où est votre mère? Est-elle entrain de baiser ce soir? Il sera facile de la trouver. [*Tr: Where is your mother? Is she fucking men tonight? It will be easy to find her.*]

NANCY:
You know, it's perfectly natural to be attracted to someone, Don, but I'm not entirely sure that this is the best way of expressing it.

NANCY [*to* JANE]:
Would you like me to toss those in the dryer for you? I think the dampness may have been part of the attraction.

JANE:
Thank you, but I think I need to go.

DON [*to* JANE]:
Tell you what I think happened. What it was is, I saw them lying on the floor . . .

ETIENNE:
Tok to di sojas, Auntie. I don'
know nutin' 'bout it.

NANCY:
Oh, Don. Don't make it any
worse.

DON [*to* NANCY]:
You know something? All I *do.*
All I've done the past twenty-
four hours. Try to do something
for a couple of people, outa the
goodness of my heart, and here
you come along with some
ridiculous little misinterpretation.

NANCY [*to* JANE]:
Would you like us to drive you
somewhere?

DON:
She's got nowhere to *go,* Nance.
Where the hell's she gonna go
at—? [*Looking at his watch*]
Goddamn this watch!!

[*During the preceding,* SOLDIER 2 *has found* ETIENNE'*s CD player in
his backpack. At* AUNTIE MIMI'*s instigation, he has placed the headphones on* ETIENNE'*s head and secured them with a rubber band.*]

AUNTIE MIMI [*to* SOLDIER 1 *and* SOLDIER 2]: Allez-y. [*Tr: Go ahead.*]

[*The CD player is switched on with the volume loud enough that the
audience can plainly hear it.* ETIENNE *writhes and turns his chair over
as* SOLDIER 1 *and* SOLDIER 2 *laugh.*]

ETIENNE: Auntie? No. Auntie, no no no *no no abeg abeg abeg abeg
Auntie nooooo.*

DON [*outraged*]: *What are you—? Turn that thing off!!!!*

[AUNTIE MIMI *snaps her fingers;* SOLDIER 1 *and* SOLDIER 2 *comply.*]

JANE: Okay. I *really*? I *honestly* don't believe what I have just witn—

AUNTIE MIMI: *Do* we want the information or do we *not*?

DON: Not like that. Not by hurting people.

AUNTIE MIMI [*leaning down to* ETIENNE]: Are you hurt down there?

ETIENNE: Thank you, Auntie. I enjoi di music.

AUNTIE MIMI [*barking*]: *And now you will tell us where is Father Dave!*

DON: Mimi, you are in *my* house now, you understand? This is *my* house, and in *my* house *I* am the one who makes the decisions.

AUNTIE MIMI [*folding her arms*]: Very well, Don. Go ahead then. Go ahead and make them.

DON [*kneeling down to* ETIENNE, *quietly*]: Uhh. Just . . . just help us out, son. Just— Look, I don't care what your opinion of me is. I'm just asking you to tell us what you know about Dave. Please.

AUNTIE MIMI [*amused by* DON's *approach*]: So you have decided to *plead* with him?

DON [*to* ETIENNE]: I mean, you do realize, don't you, you're not leaving people with a whole lot of options here? We're not gonna— We're just trying to solve a problem. That's all we're doing. But, c'mon now. Need you to help.

ETIENNE [*calmly*]: Biznessman? Efritin' I don tell you, I don tell you true. An' now you go fuck yuasef.

[*Pause.* DON *sighs.*]

AUNTIE MIMI: Well. This is a very interesting situation. Because here we are with the means and the opportunity to find Father Dave, but now it seems I am the only one with the *willingness* to do so. And I, the one with the least reason.

NANCY [*to* JANE]: I do think we need to find him.

JANE: Not *her* way, we don't.

AUNTIE MIMI [*condescendingly*]: Well, Miz Adams, you have not been in this situation, this *specific*, tragic situation before. And some of us have.

JANE: I don't give a shit what you've been through.

AUNTIE MIMI: Then I will assume you don't *want* to find him.

JANE: Kiss my ass.

AUNTIE MIMI: No, that is for your fiancé to do.

DOCTOR: Or not, as the case may be.

DON [*taking charge*]: All right, look. We could agonize about this 'til the sun comes up, but, since we all remember the terrible thing that happened to Father Tom—

NANCY: Which we are still not discussing.

DON [*to* AUNTIE MIMI]: I mean, it's the old carrot and the stick situation, so, so, so—

AUNTIE MIMI: But what carrot do you have, Don?

DON [*in desperation, pulling out his wallet*]:	AUNTIE MIMI:
Well, *I don't know,* is it *money*? Is that what he wants? I don't give a shit. Buy him *twenty* pairs of shoes. I mean, Jesus, we got whole *closets* full of shoes!	You think you can *pay* this boy? You cannot simply *purchase* the outcome that you want. And what do you suppose will be happening to Father Dave while you stand here negotiating the *price*?

[*Pause.* DON *puts away his wallet.*]

DON [*slowly*]: Right. Right. Right, so I guess . . . Theoretically, what I guess we're asking here is . . . whether or not there might possibly be some *way*—by which I also mean a *safe* way—

JANE: Wait. To do *what*?

DON: Some kinda . . . *incentive* to get him to . . . [*cont'd*]

JANE [*overlapping*]: Wait. *Incentive* sounds like the *stick*.

DON [*continuous*]: . . . No no no no no no no. All I'm talking about is a *way*, some *humane* way, that's all I'm asking.

AUNTIE MIMI [*to* SOLDIER 1]: Avez-vous le dispositif avec vous? [*Tr: Do you have the device with you?*]

SOLDIER 1: Bien sûr. Le voici. [*Tr: Sure. Here.*]

[SOLDIER 1 *and* SOLDIER 2 *produce black electrical stun devices from their belts.*]

AUNTIE MIMI [*to* SOLDIER 1]: Comment fonctionne-t-il? [*Tr: How does it operate?*]

SOLDIER 1: Appuyez sur le bouton. [*Tr: Press the button.*]

[*She does. A visible and savage-sounding crackle of electricity is produced.*]

JANE: *Are you fucking insane?* That's— Okay. [*Faking jauntiness*] Goodbye!

DON [*stopping her*]: Look, we want to find Dave, right? Isn't that what we want?

JANE: I'm not sure *what* you want, Don. I have some serious *doubts* about what you want.

DON: Wait a second. [*Turning*] Doctor? You've seen one of these things before, right?

DOCTOR [*calmly*]: I'm sorry, I was under the impression that I had been *fired.*

DON: Just— In your experience, would a thing like that seriously hurt a person?

DOCTOR [*laughing*]: *Would it hurt?*

DON: You know what I mean. Hurt like permanent, like, like, like—

DOCTOR: Don, we all know how this is going to turn out. If doing this thing will give you pleasure . . . [*cont'd*]

DON [*overlapping*]: *It gives me nothing of the sort!*

DOCTOR [*continuous*]: . . . then go ahead and do as you wish. Why *pretend* to ask my permission?

DON: I'm trying to do what's best for all concerned.

DOCTOR [*indicating* ETIENNE]: Not what is best for *him.*

JANE: Look, let's clear up any *confusion*, okay? Because in case you didn't know, there are certain things that we simply *do not do.* [*To* AUNTIE MIMI] All right? *We don't do that.*

[AUNTIE MIMI *snaps her fingers at* SOLDIER 1.]

AUNTIE MIMI: Venez ici. Est-ce que je peux voir ça, s'il vous plaît? [*Tr: Come here. May I see that, please?*]

[SOLDIER 1 *hands his device to* AUNTIE MIMI, *who dons reading glasses to inspect it more closely.*]

Ah yes. Here we are. [*Reading, simply*] *Made with Pride in Lansing, Michigan, USA.* [*To* JANE] None of us need to hear another lecture from *you*, or, for that matter, from *any* of you.

NANCY: Can I—? Sorry, does he really need to be on that carpet?

[AUNTIE MIMI *snaps her fingers at* SOLDIER 1 *and* SOLDIER 2.]

AUNTIE MIMI: Allez-y. [*Tr: Go ahead.*]

NANCY: It's just, being *handmade* and everything.

DON [*to* SOLDIER 1 *and* SOLDIER 2, *gesturing to the side room*]: There. Take him in there.

AUNTIE MIMI [*to* SOLDIER 1 *and* SOLDIER 2]: Amenez-le à l'intérieur. [*Tr: Take him in there.*]

[SOLDIER 1 *and* SOLDIER 2 *lift* ETIENNE, *chair and all, and carry him behind the sliding doors, which they close behind them. Pause.* DON *thinks.*]

DON [*very carefully*]: Tell you what. Not that I relish the thought of this more than anyone else, but I think we'd all agree that, if it's a question of *consensus,* that the *reasonable* thing, or at any rate, the *democratic* thing—

AUNTIE MIMI: Yes, I agree.

JANE: If *what's* a question?

DON: I mean, we could either do it as a show of hands, or—?

JANE: Okay, you're joking. Now you're joking.

AUNTIE MIMI [*all in one breath*]: So. The question is whether to proceed as necessary to learn the whereabouts of Father Dave or portions thereof. Yes means we proceed. No means we stop. I will go first. I vote yes. Don?

DON: I, uhh, okay. Well, I know people all have their individual . . . concerns, and so forth, but I do think that . . . if you balance one thing against another, in the end of all, you'd have to agree that—

AUNTIE MIMI: You are not running for office, Don.

JANE [*to* DON]: Agree with what?

DON: Agree with . . . well, that you . . . kinda gotta say yes.

JANE: I . . . I . . . I don't *believe*—

AUNTIE MIMI: Nancy?

NANCY: Yeah. Can I . . . *abstain?*

AUNTIE MIMI: Nancy abstains. Doctor?

DOCTOR: No.

DON: No?

DOCTOR: No.

DON: You sure?

DOCTOR: I am sure.

DON: Why no?

DOCTOR: Because I say no.

DON: Thought you said it wouldn't hurt like long term.

DOCTOR: My vote is no.

JANE [*to* DON]: Of *course* no. Don't even *look at me* if you think the answer is anything but *no.*

[*Pause.*]

AUNTIE MIMI: Well, this is a bit of an impasse. Here is the flaw of democracy, that it is so time consuming.

JANE: Yeah. Deal with it.

DON: All right. Back to square one.

AUNTIE MIMI [*to* DON]: Let me suggest this: allow me to transport the boy to the District Council.

JANE: If you can pry me off of him first.

AUNTIE MIMI [*losing her shit, snapping her fingers*]: Miz Adams, you have announced at least seven times that you intend to leave. [*cont'd*]

JANE [*overlapping, to* DON]: I swear to god. If she snaps her fingers at me *one more time*?!!

AUNTIE MIMI [*continuous*]: Who is stopping you? The door is open! You are free to go! [*cont'd*]

DON [*overlapping*]: Mimi? We took the vote.

AUNTIE MIMI [*continuous*]: Or, *could* it be that you would prefer *not* to leave? That in truth, you don't actually *want* to live in the way you so proudly claim that you do?

NANCY: Can I just say one thing?

[*Pause. All reluctantly turn to* NANCY.]

Or should I not?

DON: What kind of thing?

NANCY: Or does nobody want me to?

DON: No. We just. Nance.

NANCY: Then fine.

DON: What is it?

NANCY: I said fine. I said forget it.

DON: Is it *constructive*?

NANCY: *I think it is.*

[DON *gestures feebly, she continues.*]

Well.

[*She takes a deep breath.*]

I remember I used to have this little yellow Schwinn Sting-Ray bicycle. Do you remember those, with the banana seat? Well. My friend Becky Miechalk and I—

[DON *puts his head in his hands.*]

[*without stopping, to* DON] —*Fine. Then I won't speak ever again. Is that what you want?* [*cont'd*]

[*All overlap with* NANCY.]

DON:	DOCTOR:	JANE:	AUNTIE MIMI:
Just . . . just . . . *oh, for the love of god, Nance, just say whatever the hell it is you wanted to say!! Just say it!!*	Please, Nancy. Please, we just want you to finish. If you could just complete the thought for us. That is really all we are asking of you.	No, it's fine. We're listening, Nancy. Really. No one is trying to silence you, but *please*. Just finish the sentence, all right?	What *bicycle*? Why are we talking about a *bicycle*? Why do we care about a bicycle? How is this in any way applicable to the situation at hand?

NANCY [*continuous*]: *How about if I just have my vocal cords surgically removed? Huh?* [*Quietly fierce*] Dragging me off to the *armpit* of the Western Hemisphere when I could've just as easily— [*cont'd*]

DON [*overlapping*]: All I did was *sigh,* that's all I—

NANCY [*continuous*]: You know, there was a *point,* Mister, I hope you
realize, when I could've had my *pick.* Just about any man in North
America. [*Lowering her voice to a whisper*] Including one or two
I'll betcha still manage to *get it up* from time to time.

[*The overlapping has ended just in time for "get it up" to be heard.
Pause.*]

DON [*quietly*]: I think that was unnecessary.

NANCY: What were you planning to *do* with her underwear, Don? I'm
not sure I really want to know.

JANE: Nancy, *please.*

[NANCY *calms herself.*]

NANCY: All right. Well. Becky Miechalk and I were riding bikes around
the neighborhood one afternoon, and down at the end of our
block, right next to the storm drain, lying on its side was this little tiny *squirrel.* [*In baby voice*] *He wash jush a kyoot widdle biddy
skwurl.* [*Normally*] You know, just lying there and at first we
thought it must be asleep or something, but then we got closer and
we could tell that it had been, I don't know, hit by a car or something because most of its back half was sort of . . . you know.
Smushed. And I guess it must've dragged itself over to the drain
there somehow with its two front legs, and now it was just lying
there *twitching* a little, and Becky ran home, but I stood there
thinking to myself, *huh. This* is a creature *in pain,* isn't it? And I
couldn't have been more than nine or ten, but even at that age it
didn't seem right to me that anything should be made to suffer
like that, just like I don't think Dave should be made to suffer. So,
what I did was, I looked around and I found a big chunk of con-

crete and I knelt down and said a little prayer for the baby squirrel and then I just sort of dropped the chunk of concrete onto its head. Which, to this day, I still maintain was the right thing to do.

[*Pause.*]

DON: All of which means . . . what?

NANCY: All of which means . . . I think I change my vote to yes.

[*The next lines come very quickly.*]

AUNTIE MIMI: Fine.

JANE: Nancy, no. Nancy, think about it.

NANCY: I *am* thinking. I'm not *stupid.*

DOCTOR [*standing*]: Good night.

JANE [*to the* DOCTOR]: No. What are you—?

DOCTOR: I am going to sleep.

JANE: *No.* That is fucking *irresponsib*—

DOCTOR: A vote has been taken. There is nothing I can do. [*cont'd*]

JANE [*overlapping*]: That's not true. That's bullsh— [*cont'd*]

DOCTOR [*overlapping, continuous*]: You are an intelligent woman. Why do you pretend to be surprised by this? [*cont'd*]

JANE [*overlapping*]: No. No. You could— You've got to—

DOCTOR [*interrupting, with finality*]: This is what people *do.* This is what they have always done.

[*The* DOCTOR *turns to exit.*]

JANE [*following him*]: So you just *walk away*? That's your response. You don't even *care*?

DOCTOR [*from halfway down the hall*]: Good night.

[*He is gone.* AUNTIE MIMI *has opened one of the sliding doors and now confers with* SOLDIER 1. *Behind them the audience can glimpse* ETIENNE *trussed across the table.*]

DON [*to* JANE]: Can't just do *nothing*, can we? Huh? Sit here and do *nothing*, while—?

JANE: Why *not*? Why *not* nothing? [*Rapidly*] I mean, I may not be very good at articulating these things but if Dave was here. If Dave could see what is happening here, according to some supposedly *rational* calculation, justified by some kind of vague necessity, I have to believe that Dave would . . . that he— *What?!*

[SOLDIER 2 *has joined* AUNTIE MIMI *and* SOLDIER 1 *at the door. They are whispering and pointing at* JANE.]

[*To* SOLDIER 1 *and* SOLDIER 2] *You want to fuck with me, now? Is that it? Am I next? You sadists. You disgust me, you degenerate, shit-eating low-life trash.*

AUNTIE MIMI [*totally calm*]: They are asking whether or not they have seen you on television.

SOLDIER 1 [*to* AUNTIE MIMI]: C'est vrai, ouais? [*Tr: It's true, yeah?*] [*To* JANE, *haltingly*] You, uh, to be . . . is Monica Chapel, ouais?

AUNTIE MIMI [*to* SOLDIER 1 *and* SOLDIER 2, *quietly impatient*]: Oui, c'est vrai. [*Tr: Yes, it's true.*]

SOLDIER 2 [*having lost a bet*]: Ahhh, *putain de merde*!! [*Tr: God damn it!!*]

[SOLDIER 2 *reaches in his pocket and hands money to* SOLDIER 1.]

SOLDIER 1 [*laughing at* SOLDIER 2]: Ahhhhhahaha!!! Je vous ai dit ainsi, idiot! Donnez-le moi! [*Tr: Told you so, idiot! Hand it over!*] The Fa-cee-lee-tay-ture.

AUNTIE MIMI [*to* SOLDIER 1 *and* SOLDIER 2]: Bien. Assez! Allez-y. [*Tr: All right. Enough! Go ahead.*]

[SOLDIER 1 *and* SOLDIER 2 *exit through the sliding doors, shutting them.* DON *sits.* AUNTIE MIMI *remains standing.* NANCY *sits.*]

SOLDIER 1 [*from off*]: Okay okay okay, Smallie. Faut pas déconner. Que voulez-vous faire? [*Tr: Cut the crap. What's it going to be?*]

ETIENNE [*from off*]: De mes deux fesses. Je n'en sais rien. [*Tr: Kiss my ass. I don't know anything.*]

JANE [*to* DON]: I swear, I will walk out that door. You hear me? I don't have to stand for this shit.

SOLDIER 2 [*from off*]: Ce n'est pas compliqué. Nous voulons savoir où est Fada Dave. [*Tr: It's not complicated. We simply want to know where Father Dave is.*]

SOLDIER 1 [*from off*]: Ou, peut-être nous devrions demander à votre mère. Nous savons où elle est. [*Tr: Or maybe we should ask your mother. We know where she is.*]

SOLDIER 2 [*from off*]: Smallie. Dis-nous. Où peut-on trouver Fada Dave? [*Tr: Talk to us. Where can we find Father Dave?*]

ETIENNE [*from off, panicked*]: Non non non ne faites pas cela, mes amis. [*Tr: No no no don't do that, my friends.*] Abeg abeg. I say to you I don' know. I say true.

SOLDIER 2 [*from off, laughing*]: Regardez-le maintenant. Regardez la visage. Smallie, voulez-vous être héros, ou bien peut-être vous pouvez dire nous la vérité? [*Tr: Look at him now. Look at his face. Smallie, do you want to be a hero, or do you want to tell us the truth?*]

DON [*to* JANE]: Try to ask yourself. Really ask yourself, what's the best thing in the *long* run?

JANE: What about the *short* run, Don? What is it that we're doing in the *short* run?

NANCY: Does anybody mind if I turn on some music?

[NANCY *switches on a nearby radio and adjusts the dial until it plays pleasant classical music, but* ETIENNE *and the soldiers are still audible.*]

ETIENNE [*panicked, from off*]: Abeg abeg abeg. I tell you efritin', man. Je vous ai dit tout.

SOLDIER 1 [*from off*]: C'est votre dernière chance, fiston. Ne soyez pas stupide. [*Tr: Last chance, son. Don't be stupid.*]

ETIENNE [*from off*]: Je ne sais pas, casse-cul. [*Tr: I don't know, asshole.*]

SOLDIER 2 [*from off, pissed*]: Écoute, Smallie!! Fassent-nous frire vos baboules? C'est-ce que vous voulez? [*Tr: Listen up, Smallie!! Do you want us to fry your balls? Is that what you want?*]

SOLDIER 1 [*from off*]: Où est Father Dave!!? Je compte à trois: un. [*Tr: Where is Father Dave? I'm counting to three: one.*]

DON [*to* NANCY, *re: the radio*]: Maybe wanna turn that up a little?

[NANCY *turns up the volume so the music is quite loud, obscuring much of the unpleasant noises to follow.* JANE *plugs her ears.*]

ETIENNE [*from off*]: Dites-moi ce que vous voulez que je dise! Je vais le dire! [*Tr: Tell me what you want me to say! I will say it!*]

SOLDIER 1 [*from off*]: Deux! [*Tr: Two!*]

[*The horrible sound of* ETIENNE's *cries begins, fades, returns even louder, then dies out. And then it stops. When it does,* DON *turns to the sliding doors.* JANE *notices* DON *and unplugs her ears. She turns. All look expectantly toward the doors. After a few long moments,* SOLDIER 1 *emerges.* NANCY *sees him and turns off the music.* AUNTIE MIMI *goes to him to confide. All wait.*]

ETIENNE [*from off, in barely a whisper, as* AUNTIE MIMI *and* SOLDIER 1 *speak*]: Abeg abeg. No no no Mistah Soja. Pas plus, maintenant. [*Tr: No more, now.*] I don tell you efritin'.

[AUNTIE MIMI *turns to* DON.]

AUNTIE MIMI: Don?

DON: Yeah.

AUNTIE MIMI: Still nothing.

DON [*with a noble sigh*]: Ahh boy oh boy oh boy. I sure as heck don't enjoy this one bit.

AUNTIE MIMI: What shall we do?

[DON *rubs his head, thinks.*]

DON: Suppose, uhh . . . suppose we better give 'er another try.

AUNTIE MIMI [*to* SOLDIER 1]: Allez-y. [*Tr: Go ahead.*]

[SOLDIER 1 *goes back in, shutting the doors.* NANCY *turns the music back on loudly, and once again the horrible sounds begin.* JANE *leaps to her feet, grabbing* ETIENNE's *backpack by mistake. She heads for the door.*]

DON [*to* JANE, *over the music*]: Now wait a second. Now just stop.

JANE [*losing it*]: NO!! THIS IS SICK!!! WHAT WE'RE DOING IS SICK AND I WILL NOT BE A PART OF IT ANY LONGER!!! DO YOU UNDERSTAND ME?! I WILL NOT BE INVOLVED IN . . .

[JANE *gives the backpack an emphatic shake. It falls open, and something drops out—a dark plastic bag tied in a knot, containing something distinctly, well, head-shaped. It hits the floor with a sickening thunk, wobbles, then comes to rest.* NANCY *turns the music off.*]

AUNTIE MIMI [*opens the sliding door, quietly to* SOLDIER 1 *and* SOLDIER 2]: Arrêtez. Arrêtez. [*Tr: Stop. Stop.*]

[SOLDIER 1 *emerges from behind the sliding door. Quiet. Horrible pause as all stare.*]

NANCY [*standing*]: Oh god.

JANE: Wait. Whose bag is this I'm holding?

AUNTIE MIMI: Do not touch that.

NANCY: Oh god.

JANE: *Whose is this?*

DON: I think . . . think maybe that one's his.

NANCY: Oh god, Don. Oh god.

AUNTIE MIMI: No one goes near that.

JANE [*pointing at the thing on the floor*]: Okay. So then, what is *that*?

DON: Uhhhh—

NANCY: I'm gonna be sick.

JANE: *I don't know what that is.*

NANCY: I really am.

JANE: *Somebody tell me what that is.*

AUNTIE MIMI: *Stay away from that.*

JANE: I don't . . . no. I don't . . . oh no. I don't—

[JANE *starts to move toward the bag and the others shout, "No no no, keep away!" etc.* NANCY *rushes into the bathroom and slams the door behind her.* JANE *drops to her knees and begins to sob.*]

Oh god. Oh Dave. Why did they have to do that?

[DON *picks up his towel and gently drapes it over the object.*]

[*Beyond control*] *Why would they do that to Dave? Those fuckers. Dave never hurt anyone.*

[DON *kneels by* JANE, *puts his arms around her.*]

DON: Shhhhh. Easy now.

JANE: *Oh god. I have to go. I want to go now.*

DON: No no no no no. Shhhhhh. You're gonna stay right here with us.

SOLDIER 1 [*quietly, to* AUNTIE MIMI]: Madame? Que devrions-nous faire? [*Tr: Madame? What should we do?*]

AUNTIE MIMI: Don?

DON [*to* JANE, *very gently*]: But we still need to know, don't we? Still gotta know who did this. You agree with that, don'tcha?

[JANE *nods.*]

It's just something that's gotta be done.

JANE [*crying angrily*]: I hate this country. These *fuckers*.

DON: I know.

JANE: *Burn this country to the fucking ground.*

DON: But it's your call, okay? Not unless you say so. So whaddya think? Think we oughta keep going?

[*Pause.* JANE *lifts her head, nods.*]

JANE: Yeah.

DON: You sure?

JANE [*nodding resolutely*]: I'm sure.

DON [*bravely, to* AUNTIE MIMI]: Let's do it.

[AUNTIE MIMI *gestures to* SOLDIER 1, *who shuts the sliding door.* AUNTIE MIMI *turns the music back up full blast and folds her arms.* JANE *covers her ears. Above the music the audience can still vaguely hear* ETIENNE *scream.*]

ETIENNE [*from off*]: No no no no no no no abeg abeg abeg abeg abeg I tell you now. I don it. I don efritin'. Whatevah you say I don. No no no no.

[*As the music reaches a crescendo,* DAVE *opens the door and strolls in. Upon seeing him,* AUNTIE MIMI *snaps the music off.* DON *stands.*]

DAVE [*simply*]: Hey. You guys are up late.

[*He looks around for a long moment.*]

   What?

JANE: Dave?

DAVE: What's going on?

JANE: We— Where've you been?

DAVE: Down at the beach.

[*Pause. All stare.*]

Hitched a ride. I don't know. Needed to . . . think about things, so . . .

[*Beat.*]

[*With shame*] Actually, I'm kinda glad you're still up, Don, because, if you don't mind, I'd like to say something. I want to say I was outa line. No, I was. You were very kind, you were only trying to help and I was unkind in return and I have no excuse for that and, well, my faith tells me— What I mean is, that as a Christian . . . or, maybe just as a human being, I think the right thing for me to do is to ask for your forgiveness. Both you and Nancy. I just think it's appropriate for me to say that.

DON: Uhhh . . . no, sure, I . . . I mean, sure, yeah.

DAVE: Thanks. And I'm sorry. So. [*Gesturing toward the bathroom*] I, uhh . . . 'scuse me a second.

[DAVE *turns, but before he reaches the bathroom door,* NANCY *opens it. Seeing* DAVE, *she screams horribly, and then, for good measure, screams again.*]

Whoa. Didn't mean to scare ya.

[*He turns at the bathroom door.*]

Oh hey. Anybody see a red cell phone?

[AUNTIE MIMI *holds it up for* DAVE *to see.*]

Cool.

[*He shuts the door. Pause.*]

NANCY: Whoops.

[JANE *pounces on the plastic bag. The others recoil as she throws back the towel and tears it open. Inside it is nothing but a small watermelon. All stare, then* AUNTIE MIMI *opens one of the sliding doors, enters.*]

DON [*searching for something coherent to say*]: I, uh . . . I don't know, I do still contend that, uh . . . there's a . . . a fundamental . . . a responsibility that we . . . that all of us . . . uhhh . . .

[AUNTIE MIMI *returns, picks up her things.*]

AUNTIE MIMI [*briskly businesslike*]: All right, then. Don, I believe that I will see you then, on . . . Thursday, will I not?

DON: Ohh, so you will. Will indeed. Uhhh—

[AUNTIE MIMI *exits.* JANE *lies down on the bed and opens her pill bottle. It is empty.*]

NANCY: You know what's funny? I'm not even sleepy. For some reason I'm not even the slightest bit sleepy. Isn't that ridiculous? Hm. [*To herself*] What did I do with that bottle of Ambien?

JANE: Did anyone ever find that Tylenol?

DON: I mean, the thing is, you can't just *give up*. My father, you know, he was a— Time I quit the football team, remember him saying to me, why'd you *give up*? Can't be a . . . a *quitter*. Nobody likes a— You know? Can't *do* that. People don't like that.

[DON *takes off his watch and puts it to his ear.*]

Raised horses. My dad. Quarter horses. I coulda done that. Everybody likes horses.

[DON *drops the watch into a wastebasket. He turns to exit, then suddenly slumps against a wall.*]

NANCY [*moving to him*]: Donny, what's the—? *Donny?!*

DON [*whispering hoarsely*]: Get the doctor.

NANCY: *Donnnnnnyyyyy!!* [*To* JANE] *Help me. Oh god.* [*In total panic*] *Donny look at me!! Oh god* Doctor?!!! Where did he— Doctor??!!!!

[DON *drops to his knees.* JANE *does not move.* NANCY *races out of the room. A sliding door opens, and* SOLDIER 1 *emerges with* SOLDIER 2 *behind him. They ignore* DON.]

SOLDIER 1 [*sheepishly, to* JANE]: Allô, Madame? Scoozmi?

JANE [*from where she lies*]: Hmm?

SOLDIER 1: Uhhh . . . can you for mi . . . ? [*Pantomiming writing*] Can you to do dis . . . uhh?

[*He looks back to* SOLDIER 2.]

SOLDIER 2 [*quietly*]: Autograph.

SOLDIER 1: Autograph? Is not, dis thing, to be for mi? Is to be . . . for mai wife?

[NANCY *and the* DOCTOR *return.*]

NANCY: Oh god. He was just standing there and then, oh god. Oh god, I don't want him to die.

DOCTOR: He is not going to die. [*To* SOLDIER 1 *and* SOLDIER 2] Aidez-moi. Vous et votre ami. Grouillez-vous. Vite!! [*Tr: Help me. You and your friend. Come on, quick! Move it.*]

NANCY [*to* DON, *overlapping*]: Oh baby. Look at me, baby. Point to where it hurts.

DOCTOR: Everything is fine, Don. No need to worry. [*To* SOLDIER 1 *and* SOLDIER 2] Nous devons l'amener dans sa chambre. Soulevez-le. Comme ça. Soigneusement! Montre dehors! [*Tr: We need to carry him to his room. Lift him. Like this. Carefully! Watch it!*]

NANCY: Oh, Donny. I love you so much, with [*in baby voice*] *your widdle biddy faish.*

[SOLDIER 1 *and* SOLDIER 2 *lift* DON *and carry him out the door, followed by* NANCY. *The* DOCTOR *is delayed as he is about to follow.*]

JANE: Wait.

DOCTOR [*from halfway out the door*]: Yes, yes?

JANE [*holding up the pill bottle*]: I think I took the last of these.

DOCTOR: Yes?

JANE: Can you maybe get more? I'm really going to need more of it.

DOCTOR: Miz Adams, trust me, you will be fine.

JANE: No, seriously. It's— Oh, *fuck.* Would you just, *please*?

DOCTOR: My dear woman. What I gave you was *powdered sugar.* What did you *think*? I put it in a capsule, you swallowed it, that is all. And I am done with you now. If you want more, you will find it in a box in the kitchen.

[*The* DOCTOR *exits as* DAVE *enters from the bathroom. He sits on the edge of the bed.* JANE *does not move.*]

DAVE: Hey.

JANE: Hi.

DAVE: Must be sleepy.

JANE: I guess.

DAVE: Sun's coming up. Another hour.

JANE: Uh-huh.

DAVE: Better get going on that plywood. Patrice says he can handle the wiring, so. Coordinate that with him. But that floor's gonna be a big job, so. Get that under way in a couple of hours. [*Stroking* JANE's *leg*] But ummm, if you want, after that, I don't know, I was thinking, depending on how you feel, maybe we could . . . I was sort of hoping maybe we could sit down and . . . we could talk about . . .

[DAVE *suddenly covers his face and begins quietly sobbing.*]

JANE [*not moving*]: What's wrong?

DAVE: *Oh god.*

JANE: What?

DAVE: *Oh god.*

JANE: What's the matter?

DAVE: *I don't think we can get married.*

JANE: Oh. Okay.

DAVE: *Oh god I'm so scared. Please Christ Jesus help me not to be scared.*

JANE: Scared of what?

DAVE [*still crying*]: *What if we can't feel him inside of us anymore? What if he's angry at us? Oh god in heaven please don't abandon us.*

JANE: We'll be okay.

DAVE: *. . . And what if I'm gay?*

[DAVE *covers his face again and silently cries. The sliding doors open to reveal* ETIENNE. *He stares at* DAVE *and* JANE *for a moment, then turns to speak to the audience.*]

ETIENNE [*with a contemptuous snort*]: You see dat rye dere? See dat? Dat di way dey end di show.

[*He goes about collecting his things as he speaks to the audience.*]

Wha'd I tell you? Tol' efribodi frum di beeginnin'. Nobodi leesen to mi. Dey bullshit, man. Dey *is depressin'*. Make pipo *feel* bad. So now you lurn, o? You lurn yua lessen? Nest time you leesen to me. Nest time you do wha' I say to you, you *stay home.* Stay home watch sontin' on di TV. Sontin' make you feel betta.

[*He hops off of the stage and begins to make his way through the audience as lights fade onstage.*]

Okay pipo. Dass eet. All don. Play ovah. Laytz out. Timah go home.

[*He exits through the side door of the theater, letting it close with a slam. Blackout.*]

Etienne (Jon Michael Hill, *left*) challenges Dave (Brian Hutchison);
Yale Repertory Theatre production.

Auntie Mimi (Ora Jones) arrives on the scene; Yale Repertory Theatre production.

Dave (Tim Getman) confronts Auntie Mimi (Dawn Ursula); Woolly
Mammoth Theatre production.

The Doctor (Kenn E. Head) attempts to tell a dirty joke; Yale Repertory Theatre production.

Nancy (Amy Morton) cheers up Dave (Lea Coco); Steppenwolf Theatre production.

The Doctor (Kenn E. Head) and Nancy (Lisa Emery) speculate about Dave's virginity; Yale Repertory Theatre production.

Don (Paul Vincent O'Connor) and Jane (Kelly Hutchinson) get acquainted;
Yale Repertory Theatre production.

Don (Rick Snyder, *right foreground*) demands answers from Etienne
(Jon Michael Hill, *on ground*) as Soldier 1 (Chike Johnson), Soldier 2
(Adeyoye), Auntie Mimi (Ora Jones), and Nancy (Amy Morton) watch;
Steppenwolf Theatre production.